Eight Days Wonder

Recorded by
The Scribe

Drawings by
Jane Bouttell

The Larks Press

Published by the Larks Press
Ordnance Farmhouse
Guist Bottom, Dereham, NR20 5PF
01328 829207

Printed by the Lanceni Press
Garrood Drive, Fakenham

British Library Cataloguing-in-Publication Data
A catalogue record for this book is available
from the British Library

© Text The Scribe: drawings Jane Bouttell, 2000
ISBN 0 948400 95 1

This is a brief account of the Year 2000 Morris Eight Days Wonder

recorded during the event and scribed for the delight, bewilderment and amazement of those who wish to join us in our dazed and blistered recovery and share our memories.

First I should like to state that the 6 merry Morris dancers who undertook this great challenge and had the honour of preserving Will Kemp's memory DID dance the entire 132 miles from London to Norwich. The 2 musicians DID play and walk the entire route. Disbelieve all those gossips that say otherwise. The group did not stroll gaily along chatting or hitch lifts from the support vehicles to rest aching limbs, but earned the right to be remembered in Morris history as having truly completed the distance with a merry heart and much suffering.

I join them in their hearty thanks for the splendid support and encouragement of the marshals, drivers, caterers and superb Morris sides from throughout the country who saw fair play and joined in the fun.

The Long-Distance Dancers
Peter Cole, Lichfield Morris Men
Steve Conneely, Kemp's Men of Norwich
Jeffrey Evans, Brazenose Morris
Mark Jones, Golden Star Morris
David Marr, Coventry Morris Men
Dave Stewart, Kemp's Men of Norwich

The Long-Distance Musicians:
Bethan McLachlan, Golden Star Morris
Dr Uid, Golden Star Morris

The Long-Distance Support:
Tim Sercombe, Mendip Morris
Peter Salt, Kemp's Men of Norwich
Paul Mower, Mayflower Morris Men
Dave Bennett, Rumford Morris
The Scribe, Golden Star Morris
Tom Holdridge, Golden Star Morris
Howard Templeton, Golden Star Morris

Colin Sleath, Kemp's Men of Norwich (Organiser)
John Tarling, Rumford Morris (Organiser)

The First Day – Saturday 22 April 2000

Being introduced to The Chief Commoner and Yateley Highway Horse

We stay the night before the grand beginning of our journey in a scout hall at Brentwood where I arrive after travelling for what seemed like hours from deepest Norfolk, sitting sideways on a hard seat in the back of a land rover surrounded by a week's bedding and underwear. The hall smells of energetic scouts and is a busy mass of strangers. Even though we have attended a practise Kemp's Jig and Processional session in Norwich about a month previously for the sides taking part, we still are unsure who is who. Some faces of course we recognise – John Tarling is one of them. He is sitting surrounded by maps and money and paraphernalia and he recognises me!

I claim my patch of floor and clear off to the pub by dubious directions leading us past flats and shops and unfamiliar streets.

Alarm clocks are ringing and it is pouring with rain. Most people seem reluctant to get up. There are just a few eager people about. Nobody seems to have had a very good night's sleep on their blow-up beds which have been scattered around the perimeter of the hall. Dr Uid is sitting in a corner meditating and Howard says 'Good morning Dr Uid, good morning Dr Uid – my God he's not moving, is he dead?'

John Tarling is sitting at the table that stretches down the middle of the hall. He is still shuffling identity badges and programmes and instructions. John will have the daunting task of persuading tired, thirsty Morris folk out of pubs to dance a few more miles.

Catering Dave from **Rumford Morris** is cooking full breakfast complete with burnt toast. He is getting to grips with the cooker in the kitchen. A very good cup of tea at this early time of day on a Saturday.

There is a man in the ladies loo. He has taken advantage of the spare sinks as there are only three ladies at present with the group. A fair number of men trying to wash and shave in a small toilet with only two sinks is a bit of a squash. Found out who the rogue man in the ladies toilets is – I shall name that man – it is Tim, previous Squire of the Ring. He looked very embarrassed and shame-faced but the ladies will forgive him as he didn't leave whiskers around the sink.

Before we start, we assemble around John who tells us the format of the day and what we are to expect. Everyone is in fine bib and tucker and looks pristine to meet the Chief Commoner.

The support bus takes us into London – we start off in good cheer at 8.00 am. There is no one to be seen in Brentwood. I don't blame them as it is cold and wet. Who would want to get up?

Steve – 'I'm going to do the whole thing in plain capers'
Jeff – 'My feet hurt already.'

The pigeons in Valentine Park, Gant's Hill, are sitting under the trees getting dripped on. They are not moving and look very uncomfortable and soggy, rather like small clumps of mud.

The mini bus has stopped over the road from the Royal Exchange. Bells and music can be heard as we hurtle across the road. There is not much traffic. At this early hour there is only one side out to greet us as yet. The rain is less. Thank goodness we are under cover as we wait around for things to happen. It's cold. The Highway Horse from **Yateley Morris** is frolicking around amusing the small crowd. It is dancing up and down the road to the amusement of passing drivers, prancing off to visit the statue of Wellington on his horse that stands at the foot of the Royal Exchange. He seems to be having a conversation with the horse. The traffic is getting heavier now as Yateley Highway Horse gallops off into the distance and disappears.

Making music under a bin-bag

The war memorial in front of the Royal Exchange is still displaying the plastic poppies placed there. They are very soggy.

A very enjoyable dance of *Sweet Jenny Jones* performed to drum-beat by **Just William**. Other sides have arrived. The dancers from supporting Morris sides are standing by watching the performance and analysing the quality of the foot-work and style. They are rubbing their chins. The performers are looking very serious.

A television person has arrived and is taking the usual shots of bell-pads and musicians. At last the megaphone has been switched on and I can't understand a word. We are waiting around for the Chief Commoner to arrive and the long-distance dancers are impatient to get started.

A discussion on Morris footwear with Jeff, one of the long-distance Morris dancers from **Brazenose Morris**. He spotted me taking notes in the crowd and came over to introduce himself.
'I see you wear monkey boots – how much do yours cost now?'
I told him that my supplier was a pokey little shoe shop that nobody ever seem to patronise in Norwich. I think it is still open but wouldn't swear to it. I bought mine in bulk a long time ago when I first started dancing and will be hanging this pair up when I finish the distance (never say die) and going on to the next pair.
'£25 – yes they are hard to get now they are made in Yugoslavia. I get mine from a Pakistani chap off the market – They are the most comfortable footwear ever. I wear them all the time.'

The Chief Commoner is introduced. He shakes hands with the long-distance dancers. The Lord Mayor could not come. The Chief Commoner is invited to join the dancing but declines. Unfortunately he couldn't and there is loud whistling and clapping, a small speech about how wonderful it all is, and a scroll is given to John to take the to Lord Mayor of Norwich.

Two police (one man and one woman) on horse-back will escort us out of the City Of London. There is a policeman on a motor-bike also. The Highway Horse has arrived again.

Stopping at St Botolph Without Algate in the Wood of Portsoken and into the church for tea and hot cross buns provided by

Mzdemeanours Morris wearing bright pink and black kit. They are dancing for us up and down the aisles. The dancing is springy and pretty.

The church has a beautiful, purple, stained-glass window. Repairs are being done to the roof and there is scaffolding inside the church. [I asked if the kit was inspired by the colour scheme of the tiles in the toilets. Anna told me that the pink and black was chosen because these were the colour of the triangles that the homosexuals and lesbians wore in the concentration camps in the Second World War.]

There are numerous posters in the bus shelters along the route telling the people of London to vote on 4 May for the new Mayor of London.

Stepney Green Market – the fruit and veg. stall-holders are waving and smiling. A quick opportunity to collect money from an appreciative audience. The vans, cars and buses are coming very close to the dancers who are dancing along the gutter. A 26 red bus came so close I could see the colour of the driver's eyes. It was quite frightening. A busy building site to the right. An energetic labourer is standing on top of a lorry full of rubble and has begun to dance and wave his arms around.

The Land Rover (Bendover) support car has just passed us. Tom and Ted are waving out of the window. Ted belongs to Bethan the musician who takes her teddy everywhere with her.

The Highway Horse has appeared and is pressing the lights to let us cross the road to stop at the Flautist and Firkin. **Yateley Morris Men** are here to greet us. It is very hard to get a pint as there are so many Morris men in the pub and we can't get to the bar. However they are selling: **'Abbott Ale at £1.40 a pint. It is very good but only time to down one pint.'**

As it is raining so heavily outside there is dancing inside.

On our way again and Howard has jumped into the back of the support bus and is hanging out of the doors trying to take photographs of the dancers. A London taxi has just cut in between the dancers and the bus so it is rather difficult to get any shots.

There are not many people about still. Mostly traffic.

Salty and Colin are rattling collection buckets at the counter of a shellfish stall on the corner of the road and catching some people who have come out of a pub to see what the music is about.

At 11.50 am the rain has stopped. Hopefully we can all dry out now. We have left the second pub and we are approaching an underpass. The signpost says: to the left Chelmsford and to the right Dockland, Blackwall Tunnel. We have arrived at this huge roundabout. All the long-distance dancers are strutting a version of the *Shadow's Walk* while they keep warm awaiting the traffic lights to turn green and they can rush to safety.

Coming into Newham? A sculpture of girders made into what looks like sticks of rhubarb on an island in the middle of the busy main road. I can see Morris sides up ahead dancing. I guess this is where we stop. Across the road when the pedestrian lights turn to green. A sign for motorcycles to proceed as well. The Highway Horse is here to greet us. He has popped out of a shop doorway. The non-slip pink knobbles on the pavements by the pedestrian crossings are not very pleasant to dance across. They stick into Morris boots.

Dancing past the old town hall at Newham – or Stratford? – where we are to be greeted by some dignitary or other. All single file through the shoppers. With the other sides dancing behind us the procession seems to go on for ever. The *Kemp's Jig Processional* is being danced. The Highway Horse is dancing as well of course.

Many more Morris sides are here to greet us at the market. There are lady dancers wearing red who look very colourful and dazzling against the grey of the buildings. It seems they have had a good time while awaiting our arrival.

We have stopped outside the Swan at Stratford? I tried to check up just where we are, Newham or Stratford, by reading the road signs and addresses on buildings and destination of buses. No luck. Even the people I asked had different opinions. We have danced past the Social Services office and the sign on the wall says 'Stratford Branch in the Borough of Newham'.

The Highway Horse is still prancing around. There are garland dancers on the other side of the road. We are greeting and cheering each other across the road where a stream of Saturday morning traffic is moving between the two of us.

'The Swan - £2.20 a pint but it's a lot better beer. London Pride. The young man behind the bar is wearing a baseball cap back to front. The new style of bar-maids to be seen these days leaves much to be desired.'

It's 'beat the Morris dancer across the traffic lights' time coming down the Romford Road. Heading out of Stratford to *Constant Billy*. Travelling along a bus lane, which is convenient because the cars have room to get around us. A wedding party has come out to see us as we parade down the Romford High Street. The blushing bride looks beautiful in her white gown. The festivities are in full swing and it's a shame we are unable to stop and dance for her at her wedding.

Muslim ladies covered from head to foot in their yashmaks are standing outside the Imammia Mosque and peering down the road. Up the road there seems to be some sort of march with police escort. We are having to dance down the pavement because a pile-up of traffic has been caused by the demonstration or whatever is going on across the road. I have just been handed a leaflet about what is happening. There seem to be hundreds of Muslims marching - the leaflet says 'Hussain the Saviour of Islam' - lamenting and crying and beating themselves because of a tragic event in the history of mankind. The incident took place nearly 1400 years ago, and has been commemorated all over the world since.' So now we know.

There is a traffic jam in the opposite direction. This makes us feel quite pleased that we are not holding up the traffic too much on our side of the road.

It is now 1.30 pm. We left the rain behind us half an hour ago. It is absolutely wonderful Morris dancing weather. No sun out and it's cool. The procession has now changed to *Brighton Camp* from *Constant Billy*. The traffic is really heavy now but people must be used to weird things happening around the London area as they seem to take us in their stride.

Coming into Ilford. The processional has changed to *Black Joke*. We are sending the support bus on ahead to find a place to meet us for lunch. A bit frightening really as it was a big lump of metal behind us protecting us from the traffic. Into Ilford town centre. It's a precinct. The Morris sides are here waiting for us and dancing. There are no cars, but there are crowds of people. Hopefully we can collect a lot of money. We finished this stretch outside the Home Furnishing Store.

'A quick gallop past the perfume counter and swim-wear and up the escalator to the fourth floor and to the toilets. Very clean and tidy they are too.'

Other people have dived into McDonalds' loos and have come out with rather disgusting-looking coffee in bendy, squashy cardboard cups. Out come the sandwiches and crisps, apples and Penguin biscuits. The catering wagon had a problem catching up with us here as no cars are allowed in the precinct.

We are greeted by **Chingford Morris** who have a spectacular ram as their animal. He really looks good with his golden horns. There is hardly any time to stop here and eat or chatter to **Chingford Morris**. We are feeling cold now we have stopped.

Leaving Ilford at 2.20 pm. It's not raining but it is cold. Hopefully we will warm up soon. We have left the **Romford** side behind. They are still dancing in the precinct. The long-distance dancers are going on by themselves.

Tolgate Tavern a mile or so down from Romford.

'The beer is not bad in here. £1.90 so it's not bad. Cheaper than Norwich prices.'

Leaving the Tolgate Tavern at 3.30 pm. A mile into Romford for our next stop and meeting the next Morris side. Dancing *Constant Billy* into Romford. One of the young ladies from **Mzdemeanours** has come to join us. The dancers are waving hankies and leaping and jumping at the speed cameras. **Romford** has some very aggressive drivers. A motor-cyclist swerved to overtake us on the wrong side of a traffic island. We are occasionally sworn at by drivers and it seems the sport of the day is 'playing skittles with the Morris side'. Very loud thump-thump music can be heard from the cars. The buses are belching out black fumes. I am sure this is terribly unhealthy. A crowd of Asian lads at the bus stop are dancing to our music, which cheers us up tremendously, but when invited to dance with us they refuse.

Entering Romford market place. Dancing around the bollards. Crowds of people are assembled to welcome us, Union Jacks flying from stalls, shouting and applauding. There is great enthusiasm and a raucous welcome from the people of Romford. **Royal Liberty Morris** are here in their distinctive costume. Scraggy, a woman from **Royal Liberty Morris**, has run to greet us beating a drum and leaping into the air. **Royal Liberty** looks a riot. The musicians are splendid. They are dressed as rams, crow and stags. Their custom is extremely tatty and they play the pipes. Their molly is something to behold. He is a large man with whiskers and black face, dressed up as an old woman. He has a smile that lights up his whole face.

The Highway Horse is back dancing amongst the crowd. He just pops up in the most unlikely places. At the moment he is bowing and nudging and making a nuisance of himself in the crowd. He is very popular with children and adults alike.

The Golden Lion – 'The beer is OK. Drinking Old Peculiar. I asked the bar-maid for an Old Peculiar and she asked me for my phone number.'

A wonderful send-off from **Royal Liberty**. Promises to see us all later in the year for a party. We have remade old friendships and interesting yarns are being regurgitated to the delight of those who are listening.

It is raining again and we are dancing to *Queen's Delight* as we leave Romford. It has been decided to dance a round-about way out of Romford and so we are dancing into and through a residential area. An odd supermarket or two dotted around. Speed-calming humps across the middle of the road. These are upsetting the rhythm of the dancers. Legs are now getting tired. The manhole covers are very painful to dance over and there seem to be a tremendous number of them round here.

4.45 pm and nobody about in this built up area. They must have all done their shopping and settled down for the night and tea.

'Gidea Park' it says on the tube station wall. All the Indian Takeaways are starting up for the rush on a Saturday night. A definite whiff of curry in the air.

At the Shepherd and Dog about half an hour later than planned. The musicians from **Royal Liberty** are here to wave us in. They are drumming and piping very loudly. While we are having refreshments they are playing in the car park. It makes us feel we haven't been forgotten and it has perked us up no end to see them. What splendid comradeship.

'A nice fruity pint of Adnams at the cost of £2.'

A fond farewell from **Royal Liberty** musicians and we are dancing on our way to *Constant Billy*. Into the countryside and past Tylers Common. It is now drizzly rain and the road is very narrow so we are having to go single file. There are big expensive houses on route. Summer is a-coming in, the bushes are all in bud and the plastic garden furniture is out. Dancing along the fly-over of the M25. The queue of traffic heading into London is horrendous. The traffic coming out of London is sparse but going at great speed. I wonder what the drivers are thinking looking up and seeing a procession of Morris dancers waving hankies and prancing overhead. 'Guess what we saw on the way here tonight?'

Have just been informed that the enormous Brentwood Hill that John told us about at our breakfast meeting is ahead. All the sides we spoke to throughout the day said, 'You're not going up that awful hill are you?' when they heard about the planned route. I am feeling rather apprehensive about all this. The traffic has given way to us dashing across the main road. The drivers are all waving. The hill is ahead! I don't like the look of it at all. *Winster Processional* is being played with vigour spearing us on. It's dusk now and the cars have their lights on.

Well that wasn't as bad as I thought. Like going to the dentist – the thought of it was worse than the actual event. Mind you, it wasn't a picnic by any means. Looking forward to a nice cup of tea now.

It's wet and windy. We are stopping in a small shopping precinct in Brentwood at the end of the first day. It seems a very grey ending to the day's adventures. A small group is here waiting to welcome us.

They are brave souls for hanging around in this weather. A few dances being performed by the local sides and on to the mini bus and back to the hall. Everyone soaking their feet as best they can in surgical spirits. We are all cold and the floor heating has only just been turned on.

Trying to decide where to go for something to eat - pub/chippy/Chinese/Indian takeaway. Showers and baths are out of the question as there are only four sinks between us all and these are being used to wash socks. Everyone is counting the number of blisters they have accumulated during the first day. Not too many as yet, just sore knees.

I go with the Druid gang from Norwich to try and find somewhere warm and inviting to eat and drink. Although Brentwood is pretty by night with a wonderful laser display stretching into the sky no hostelry takes our fancy. We go into the car park of the Artichoke but there are so many cars that we decide we don't want to queue. We are just too tired to appreciate anything I guess. Decide on picking up a Chinky takeaway and eating it back in the hall. We are so tired we eat in silence and then tumble into our blow-up beds. [I was so stiff, Tom had to lift me out of Bendover.]

Those who went to The Artichoke said: **'Bass very nice, but a Toby pub and uninteresting. Went on to Flying Fish Chippy - mushy peas - not mushy enough but chips very nice. Then on to the Essex Arms - Adnams OK but sharp. Under £2 a pint. Should have tried Youngs Special. Pam's Bar - music too loud - then on to the Horse and Groom. Old Speckled Hen. £2.10 a pint but very nice. Kicked out after closing time.'**

Dave S. feet gave him so much pain tonight that he had to crawl to his bed on his hands and knees. I shall be very surprised if he will be able to stand on them tomorrow. They have swollen up.

The Second Day – Sunday 23 April 2000

A good deed and polkaing around the flower beds

Dave is up and about and walking in a very peculiar fashion.

We dance away from the London Marathon, which starts today. Colin S. is awake bright and early and sitting at the breakfast table in his Morris kit and reading a newspaper. He looks like a Headmaster as he peers over the top of his spectacles at the rabble emerging from their beds.

Dr Uid is roaming around the hall delivering cups of tea to those still in bed. The sun is shining. It can be seen through the high slit windows. There is no ceiling in the scout hall, only the rough skeleton of the rafters. It rained so hard last night that it sounded like frogs hitting the roof. It felt rather like being in the ark.

I was sorting my kit out this morning and wondering if I could get away with wearing my Morris socks for a second day. Found I had worn the soles completely out of my socks. No wonder my feet are smarting.

Howard is cleaning his Army boots. They look very impressive – all set for a route march.

Arrive back in Brentwood. The sun is still shining and it is a glorious morning. The church bells are ringing. The new Roman Catholic Cathedral is as beautiful in daylight as it is at night. Wish we had time to have a look inside. Another place to return to after the event.

General chit-chat and joviality with the Mayor of Brentwood. We are standing around the 'Pious Memory of William Hunter, Native of Brentwood 1861 Memorial' for posed photo. There is a presentation of yet another scroll to add to the collection to be handed to the Lord Mayor of Norwich.

Blackmore Side are dancing with us out of Brentwood at 10.05 am to *Winster Processional*. Stop at traffic lights to take off coats and jackets

The **Blackmore Morris** are galloping along at the front of the long-distance dancers setting a cracking pace. Perhaps too strenuous to begin with.

Coming out of Brentwood. On the left-hand side there are little boys sitting in the trees watching us. There is a football match in the field. Rows of mums and dads are standing on the touch line encouraging their offspring.

The gardens of the houses are glorious with an abundance of magnolia in bloom. Some daffs have survived the frost. People have started to come out of their houses to wave.

A few drivers are getting very angry. They can't get between the dancers and the traffic islands in the middle of the road. They are not waiting and swerving to overtake on the other side of the road.

First stop at the Rose at Shenfield for liquid refreshment, tea only, pub not open. Pretty little pub with tables and benches outside, it's a pity patrons sit by the main road though. At the moment the long-distance dancers are missing the omnibus addition of the Archers. For those fans who are interested – Sid is enjoying the delights of Jolene and the Grundies are complaining about how hard-done-by they are, living in a flat. Liz and David at loggerheads over their parents' money. All is about to explode. Keep listening.

The marshals are having quite a job keeping the traffic under control. The islands in the middle of the road on this long stretch of road are causing chaos and the traffic is building up.

The big roundabout crossing over the A12 is potentially dangerous. Marshals at every junction advising the drivers and dancers to beware of each other. Salty is way ahead waving his arms about. He is a treasure. Colin coming up the rear and doing a magnificent job also. Tim is darting between the front and the back at quite a trot. He must have covered miles by now. These three seem to be forgotten about as they are never around the main body of the activity. Before I forget – thanks a lot.

Stopping at The George and Dragon at Mountnessing. The pub is not open so the Morris men are using the garden to relieve their bladders.

Black Bull Morris have come to join us outside the pub. **Blackmore** are dancing. Lots of mobile phones around at this stop. Time to catch breath and report back to the family.

Left The George and Dragon with the musician from **Blackmore** taking his dog for a walk. Taffy the dog is watering the daffs but is very well-behaved and not under the feet of the dancers. He is sniffing at all the trees and bushes as we walk past them. The marshals are racing into paper shops along the route to see if we are mentioned in any of the newspapers. We appear in most of the local papers and also in *The Guardian*.

At Truelove's Lane outside Ingatestone the tune has changed to *Brighton Camp*. We are travelling down the working side of the road works and out the other side dancing to *Oyster Girl*.

Dancing through the suburbs. The only people on the roads seem to be those going to the local garden centres.

Stopped at Ingatestone at the Star. **Black Bull** side ready to dance. **Rumford Morris** dancing as well.

A very quiet 'do'. No pub open yet. A round of applause for the long-distance dancers as they arrive. **Black Bull** gave all the members and their support a blue or red silk rose. These are being pinned to hats and baldricks and waistcoats. **East Saxon Sword Rapper Side** are dancing nice and tight. I am told they dance at 160 steps a minutes. This means nothing to me except that they look jolly amazing. Apparently they are working up to 180 steps a minute. All agree they are very professional. We are most impressed and well entertained. What I can't get over is how their kit is neatly pressed – They look as if they have just taken it off the hanger of the laundrette. A small crowd of people have gathered. I think they are mostly relatives.

'The Star – The Abbott Ale is exceptional, straight from the barrel. Enjoyed in front of an enormous log fire at £2.05 a pint. IPA was good as well at £1.90 a pint. There is a mynah bird in the pub who is very noisy and coughs a lot. Fire so big it takes up most of the pub.'

Left Ingatestone and arrived at Margaretting. The same people are here to greet us.

'The Black Bull – very nice atmosphere in pub, traditional English. Cheese and onion rolls and veggy food on the bar. No meat in sight. Very pleasant landlord. Ridley IPA at £1.90 a pint. Exceptionally nice especially after dancing up hill.'

The landlord's name is Kirk. The shelves in the lounge part of the pub are full of medals and trophies won at darts.

Leaving the Black Bull and around the roundabout. A profusion of bum bags and mobile phones are bouncing around on the hips and bottoms of the long-distance dancers. Morris has moved into the 21st Century.

'The White Horse – plastic, modernized, typical Big Steak pub. Beer – Marstons Pedigree at £2.18 a pint. Very new and needs another day to be at its best.'

We are travelling down the underpass to Moulsham. Dancing into Oakland Park and stopping outside the Chelmsford and East Sussex Museum/Essex Regiment Museum. The weather is typical of an early summer's day and we are having an ice cream stop. Everyone races into the museum to visit the loo.
'Through the lovely old building and along a corridor, past exhibits to the toilets which are lovely and clean.'

The staff at the museum are extremely friendly. Outside the museum, the gardens are at their best. The tulips are a brilliant red. The Morris men are having a quick polka around the flower beds.

Out of the park to *Hunt the Squirrel*.

Arriving at the Meadow Mall in Chelmsford. This seems to be built in between the River Chelm and the canal. **Black Water North West Clog side** are dancing. A passer-by is so taken with the dancing that he has tripped over a large flower pot that stands outside a coffee shop.

Three members of the long-distance dancers are busy leap-frogging the bollards by the bridge while waiting to be introduced to the Lord Mayor who has just arrived looking very sleek in a pale-coloured suit.

The local radio people are interviewing John.

The sun is going behind the clouds and there is a chill in the air.

Dave Fuller and his daughter Clare Fuller are dancing a jig together. The maid is wearing a mob cap, green knitted shawl and long black skirt. She looks very coy. They dance very well together and are smiling all the time they are dancing.

A reading from the diary of Will Kemp by John Tarling about the day the young maiden danced with him in Chelmsford.

Howard is keeping quite a record of events with his camera. He tells me that while we were waiting for the Lord Mayor to arrive he realised that he had run out of film and was anxious to take a photo of Dave and Clare dancing together. He spied an Argos store which was open and ran frantically around trying to find some film. The manager came to his assistance and when he heard why Howard needed the film he tossed him a packet containing three films and said 'on the house' - an example of the spirit of most of the people we have met.

The gentleman who tripped over the plant pot is filling out an accident report form whilst having a cup of tea.

We are dancing out of the very busy shopping area. Tesco is open (24 hours). Cars are coming in and out of the parking areas in all directions. Shopping trolleys are being shoved out of the way and are stored at random. I guess people are fed up with having to shop on a Sunday instead of relaxing.

Bromesfield: pretty little village. Getting into pargeting country again. Very simple designs on the buildings. There is a back-log of traffic as the dancers arrive in the village. What a surprise! - met Nigel and Sarah who danced with a molly side in Norwich before they moved to this part of the country. They did not know that we would be going past their house and we did not know that they were so close. A fond greeting and a promise to meet up at the pub later.

A stop at the Angel. **'Yet another Big Steak pub. Quite a sizeable range of real ale. Adnams £2.05 a pint. Pleasant after the last pub and drinking Bodingtons in a Mates Wine Lodge (by Mall in Chelmsford at £1.10 a pint). Fruit machines decorate the walls. Olde Worlde type décor.'**

There is music and dancing at the pub. Food is traditional pub grub and expensive. Soaking the daffs and cowslips in a pint of beer and picking off the petals to eat while we wait to eat. Are we really that hungry? The beer-soaked flowers taste remarkably good. Jugs of beer on the house.

Rumford Morris Men bid us a fond farewell at The Angel. They have been very supportive and friendly companions these last 2 days and we shall miss them.

A very leisurely time eating and resting our feet. A sign on the door states 'No working clothes or boots'. So we all take our boots off and steam.

The two friends from Norwich have arrived at the pub. They have cycled here. Plans are being made to meet again later in the year in Norwich.

Transported by the support vehicles back to the scout hall. Silly songs and stories are being told on the mini bus. Mark has sat on Steve's lap all the way back. They both look very happy with the arrangement. As the bus retraces our steps back to the hall the distance does not seem so very far.

A little ditty about a vicar and a choir-boy was sung by Tim on the bus driving back. Tim thinks it was first sung by Jake Thackray but nobody knows for certain.

Now we have arrived back at the hall, feet are being soaked in buckets and socks are being washed. Some people are going to visit the pub tonight. Some are having an early night. It will be good to sleep in a proper bed tomorrow night and get off these blow-up beds.

Ted has been sellotaped to the support van window and has been enjoying the view all day. Somehow these dastardly Morris men kidnapped Ted and used him for soft furnishings in the van. Bethan is not at all pleased and there is a yukky reunion.

The Third Day – Monday 23 April 2000

An argument about eggs and meeting a blind man

It rained heavily in the night. It woke every one up. 7.00 am 'Next year we do this on the Internet' was the suggestion put forward this morning as feet were being tended to.

Breakfast was prepared in the usual confused order. Dave had two helpers in the kitchen turning sausages and burning the toast. They are doing a fine job though. As usual the veggies are sticking to toast and cereal. A request for scrambled eggs. Catering Dave has just produced boiled eggs for the veggies, served up in the cardboard egg cartons. They are cooked to perfection and nice and dippy for soldiers. Jovial banter about slicing the top off the egg or peeling the shell. Peeling won (because I say so). At the end of the egg the Druid family insist that holes are bashed in the bottom to prevent the witches from floating in them on water. This is a custom from Lowestoft.

Dr Uid has gone down a notch in his trousers and is busy digging into his belt to make another hole.

It's starting to rain quite steadily again. We are packing up the vehicles. There seem to be more going into the vehicles than we came with. We are having quite a squash to get in. John has phoned for help to get us to our starting point. We are starting away from the hall on time which is very surprising. Everyone is beginning to look like they have danced for 30 odd miles now. What a difference the weather makes. If it were sunny we would be much more cheerful and our feet wouldn't seem to hurt so much.

It is pouring with rain as we negotiate the rush hour traffic in the support vehicles taking us back to the spot we left yesterday. John is worrying about his straw hat getting wet.

Warming up in the car park before we start out. A lively session of *Bleddington*. There is a long procession of school children dawdling to school by the pathway at the back of the pub. A great long crocodile procession with their satchels and packs. There are some parents at the back escorting them and chatting amongst themselves. Colourful umbrellas. They don't seem to have spotted us.

Starting off going across the zebra crossing with the orange lollipop lights flashing. The time is 9.33 am. Off we go.

Dancing on the pavement because the traffic is so heavy. Because there has been so much rain our hankies are flicking all the water off the bushes and we are getting wet. Trotting along now to *The Rose*.

Coming out into the countryside, leaving behind the awful pedestrian non-skid knobbles that hurt our feet. The sun has come out and it is getting warm. Jackets are being handed to the marshals and on we go.

The Lollipop Man and *Constant Billy* as we go along the road to Braintree. We are now out on to the dual carriageway. Away from the built-up area and the scenery is quite boring. Down the A131 to the tune of *Brighton Camp*. A bit of muck-spreading going on here - the nice smell of the countryside.

First stop in the lay-by. Lots of aches and pains, injuries and blisters. They really took on a cracking pace to this spot. The marshals had to jog to keep up with the dancers all the way. They won't be able to keep this pace up for the rest of the day. The tune changed several times to slow things down. The music cannot be heard at the back of the procession because of the traffic noise. The dancers are taking it in turn to pace at the front.

Dr Uid is again being strapped into his squeeze box. He has to have this tied on for comfort. Away we go. Out of the lay-by to *Brighton Camp*. A beautiful clump of narcissi growing around the signposts on the way in and out of Chatham Green. The squire of **Peterborough Morris** joins us for this stage of the journey. The roads are down to two lanes. Some very nasty bends. The traffic is quite frightening.

Great and Little Leighs. Going up hill along the pavement and flicking the rain off the trees and bushes although the sun is coming out again. Yvonne, the fiddle-player from **Fleet Morris,** who has been with us the entire journey so far has a sore hip. Her fingers are cold and sore but she is still cheerful.

Dancing into the Dog and Partridge at 11.18 am.

The Dog and Partridge – 'The landlord opened especially half an hour early. Two and a half pints of an exceptionally nice Ridleys IPA. 3.5% but very nice and an extremely nice landlord. £1.90 a pint.' In this pub I was told there was a partridge that was vicious.

Well-wishers, Mr and Mrs Crossman of Great Leighs came to greet us as they heard about the event on Radio Essex – 'I thought I would come along on Monday because after the weekend's support enthusiasm is a bit low and we thought we would come and give a bit of moral support.'

Dancing away from the Dog and Partridge to *Black Joke*. The time is 11.50 am. Howard is playing his shells at the back of the procession so the dancers can hear the beat of the dance.

The wind is very strong and blowing the dancers into the hedgerows. A lot of cheerful encouragement amongst the dancers to keep their spirits up.

Changing to *Vandals* as the sun comes out and it is lovely and warm but the pavement is a bit dicey as it has had a lot of repairs. We are dancing around potholes. The Morris dancers have their shadows dancing with them along the road. This would make a splendid photograph. I wonder if Howard thought so too. At least the road has straightened out now. No more hills. Coming into Braintree. A brief lunch stop in a lay-by. Deborah Corham lives at the side of the lay-by and kindly opens her house up for us to go to the loo.

We have a Morris man coming to join us. He is from **Peterborough Morris** and is married to Sally who is a direct descendant from Will Kemp. Sally is coming to greet us later today and join in the celebration. Apparently they have a book that the family have written about Will Kemp and their history.

We have been told the local paper in Thetford has written an article about us arriving there on Thursday. I hope Thursday is pension day so they have some money to donate to our efforts.

Overtaking a queue of traffic. The road works lights ahead are on red. Going quicker than the average car! What a difference the sun makes when it comes out, everyone seem livelier and brighter. The musicians seem to have cheered up. It is really pleasant now and we are forgetting our aches and pains.

Brocking and Braintree. We are dancing down the tree-lined pavement towards a blind man coming up the hill with his white stick tapping along in front of him. He has just walked straight down the middle of the procession. Goodness knows what he is thinking as we swerve around him. From the moment we met him to the time when the last dancer passed him his face never altered expression. No smile or bewilderment on his face. He never faltered on his journey.

Catering Dave doing a grand job as usual dishing out the sandwiches and fruit and choccy biccies. We are all sitting in the lay-by on the grass. Bums are getting wet. At least our feet are getting rested. Dr Uid sits there looking rather dashing in his King's Army outfit, which he uses for his Morris kit.

Away from the lay-by with wet patches on our britches and going into Braintree to *Hunt the Squirrel*. The collection buckets are out and hopefully we will get quite a bit of money in Braintree. 1.05 pm

The marshals have gone on ahead as there are road works and the traffic signs have to be re-shuffled to allow us past. They are quick to put all the signs back again when we have passed by.

Into Braintree town. Those knobbly pink pedestrian non-slip paths again. They really do cut through the soles of shoes. Howard is playing the shells again as we arrive. They can be heard very clearly.

Here we are splitting up and visiting various shops and pubs. Howard runs off to buy another pair of shoes as the Army boots he is wearing hurt his feet. Medical supplies are replenished. One or two people are hanging around with bags of shopping wanting to see some dancing but we are too sore to oblige and want to have some liquid refreshment. If they hang on a bit longer for us to reassemble I am sure that John will perform a jig.

'White Horse at Braintree – IPA – half pink - £1.16. IPA is very nice and the landlord's name is Richard, a very friendly chap who gave us a drink on the house. The people in the pub were very chatty and friendly and wanted to know about what we were doing. A very nice pub.'

'The White Hart in Braintree – the landlord was extremely nice. He gave us a free pint each for the dancers who sat there. Extremely nice pub – very posh – far too posh to let the likes of us in.'

Dancing through the shopping precinct of Braintree on the way out of the town to the *Winster Processional*. A collection of youths have joined us on the end of the dance line. They are laughing and waving their arms but unfortunately they only last a few yards before they give up and go on their way. We told them to do at least a mile but they were too out of puff to answer.

Coming out of Braintree pedestrian precinct and past beautiful well-kept houses on Bradford Street. They look old enough for Will Kemp to have danced past. There are cobbles Cascading down the driveways from the houses and small alleyways. Peeking up the alleyways to see yet more tiny little cottages in a festoon of colours and garden plants. The houses here are a delight to go past and it takes your mind off your aching limbs. The old houses are exceptionally well kept on this road out of Braintree. It's a shame that the telegraph poles and television aerials get in the way of the beautiful view. Absolutely wonderful. It is obviously bin day as there are filled black bin-liners lining the streets and the marshals are running ahead hurling them off the path.

A short unplanned break and off we go again to the tune of *Vandals* after mending a violin string. The wood-carvings on the houses are absolutely beautiful. It is really a very pleasant place. 1.45 pm

Howard has spotted a litter bin with the lid removed and is dancing alongside with

'..like a mobile salt-pot..'

the cover over his head. His hands can just been seen waggling about out of the bottom of the cover. His eyes are peering out of the slits. He looks like a mobile salt pot. He has eventually abandoned the cover further down the street and has a black smudge on the top of his head.

Lay-by at Hedingham for a short break and on we go again to *Trunkels*. Stopping at Hare and Hounds for a fifteen minute break at 3.05 pm. **'Abbott Ale - £2.15 a pint. Extremely nice. Nice wood floor – pleasant pub – landlord's name – Nigel. The landlord has only been in this pub for three weeks. He is usually closed at this time of day but decided to keep his pub open all day even though he didn't know we were going to arrive.'**

Everyone sitting around the pub comparing blisters and not really wanting to take their shoes off and see what damage they have done to their feet. Socks are being changed for more comfort. All agree that this is a tough day.

Starting off again from this wonderful pub where we have had such a good welcome. 3.15 pm. We have been told there are seven miles to go. The tune is *The British Grenadiers*. We are beginning to look a bit the worse for wear and some of the dancers are not in entirely official kit but are feeling a bit more comfortable.

A short détour off the route to dance around the forecourt of Foley House and wave to the people who have come to the windows to watch. They are waving and taking photographs. This is a residential home for deaf people. As we dance past the high wall that circles the House we are jumping up high, waving our hankies over the top of the wall so they can see the hankies going by from the windows.

The local people around here are very very friendly. They are bibbing their horns and racing out of their homes to take our photograph and waving to us and cheering us on our way. It is nice when you are getting tired to get enthusiasm to spur you on.

Entering Gosfield at 3.30 pm. The weather is really lovely but there are clouds forming. Stopped at the King's Head. 3.50 pm. We are 2 minutes early! The King's Head is shut so we are diving into the Lucozade and bananas and muesli bars. There is some nice pargeting on the King's Head pub wall. It's a shame it isn't open. There are a few people here to see us. We have sold some programmes and souvenirs. The people are all smiling.

We have to negotiate around some road works. Dancing on the pavement on the right hand side of the road. John says there is just under five more miles to go until we stop for the evening. We are all looking forward to hot showers.

Single file down the pavement. A uniform springy swagger with a few hops in-between. The dancers are very tired and the musicians have set a tough pace again. The musicians have been absolutely marvellous since we started. No complaints from them. They just get on with it. Yvonne the fiddle player is very good. The other musicians have a lot of respect for her. Bethan is the recorder player and is holding the pace well even though she is a tiny little thing. She is always jolly and smiling and a delight to have with us. Dr Uid is on the squeeze box – it's a heavy instrument to carry after a time. I know it is hurting his back but he is cheerful as always.

The road surface is hard to dance on. It is gritty and it hurts the soles of the feet. The evening is lovely, the sun is shining and it is cool and perfect Morris-dancing weather.

Howard is forever taking photographs. This takes the biscuit – he is driving the mini bus whilst at the same time taking interesting photographs of the dancers who are dancing backwards and waving to him, while Tim is walking alongside with his arm through the driver's window working the steering wheel.

Coming into Sible Hedingham twinned with Choisy-au-Bac at 4.25 pm. This is the most uncomfortable road surface to dance on. We can see the castle in the distance and are creeping towards it. The pargeting on the houses here is really wonderful. Suns, moons, flowers, horses, fans - very pretty in this quaint village. We are stopping off at The Swan Inn for a brief rest until we start off on the last leg.

The Swan Inn 'Most upsetting – the Old Bailey's Strong Beer has just gone so I will have to make do with a pint of £1.80 Greene King IPA which is the worst brewery in the world. But the pub is extremely civilized with a lot of chesterfields around and the company is very civilised.'

There is a penny-farthing bicycle hanging over the huge inglenook fireplace. Sally (Kemp's descendant) has joined us in this pub. They have been out with the collection buckets all day to help with our expenses.

Left the Swan Inn at 5.10 pm. Turning down out of the village into pretty country lanes, over the bridges and we are nearly at the end of this day. Coming into Castle Hedingham to the tune of *Kemp's Jig*. We are all very tired.

Into the Bell. The landlord has arranged food especially for us. We can order now and then settle into the youth hostel, shower and return.
'The ladies' loos in the Bell are absolutely astonishing. They are wonderful. Beams and blue and white tiles, marble wash stands. So interesting. I would move into this loo.'

The pub is so unusual. There are narrow corridors leading to small rooms and eating areas. Low beams and uneven floors. Lovely.

Morris in the Maze have met us at this pub. They are very friendly and wet because they have waited for us in the rain. The rain has held off all day and its just beginning to fall.

Across the road to the youth hostel and showers! The rooms are serviceable, clean and the beds are comfortable. Oh dear! Only one shower working. How unfortunate that some dancers have to queue for the showers in the pub and do some more drinking while waiting.

Back over the road and into the pub after a shower. Other sides have arrived. **Belchamp Morris** have taken up an entire room of the pub. They are singing and dancing. The pheasant feathers in their hats brush the ceiling. The pub is heaving with merry people, chatting, meeting friends, singing. The food is passable but nothing to write home about. However, they did put on the food especially for us. A quick visit to the wonderful loo before returning to the youth hostel and a comfortable bed.

Tucking up early with a cup of tea. The end of a gruelling day. The road surfaces were appalling – very stony. Up tomorrow bright and early.

The Bell – 'This has five stars which makes it the top pub of the tour up to now. The oak beams! No juke box, no fruit machines, Spitfire? Sheping? brew which is one of the best breweries in the country. The ambience (big word – not one of those things with the flashing light on) excellent. I don't know how much the beer is because I have just had this bought for me.'

Howard – 'What is most famous about Castle Hedingham is the Norman keep. It's the largest one of its kind in England, and it's a real shame that we are not going to be able to visit it. The pub is absolutely amazing. It's in a world of its own. The whole village looks really lovely and I am going to come back here again.'

Well it's obvious from the various comments about the Bell that it is a very popular place. It is well worth a visit and we should all like to return when we have more time.

I am sitting with my meal accompanied by Sally Stevens and her husband – this is what she nervously told me, using my dictaphone:

'Hello I'm Sally Stevens, descendent of Will Kemp. I have come out today to join them on a Monday and I shall be out again on Thursday in Thetford with some other members of the family I hope. My grandmother was Violet Kemp. She came from a large family most of whom spent their lives out in India and Burma. I believe my second cousin's brothers, Richard and John, are the last of the Kemps. My grandmother Violet Kemp married a man who lived not far from here. My grandfather is buried a few miles away from Sible Hedingham. He married Violet Kemp. I feel there must be some connection with this area. So I think Will Kemp must come from around this area. Our family connections in Norfolk is in Norwich and even, I believe, in King's Lynn - very early on in King's Lynn. We think he might have been born in Finchingfield, son of John Kemp. I didn't know that I was descended from Will Kemp until my mother died three years ago when I met my second cousin for the first time who was May Kemp. I wasn't born a Kemp. She told me that she actually have seen the family history book which was written by a family member about 1900. All the family members in the past was mentioned and Will Kemp was one of them. I don't know how well researched it was but it was actually written in this book.'

The Fourth Day – Tuesday 24 April 2000

'Will Kemp – I hate the man'

Much rubbing of limbs and putting on plasters and surgical wraps. We are all still in good cheer but realise that we have another day's dancing ahead of us. The sun is shining.

Dave S. is up with the larks doctoring his feet. After a few painful steps he begins to walk fairly well. He is determined to complete the journey.

A civilized breakfast sitting at long tables. First, the queue for a choice of apple/orange juice. Cups and saucers, butter pats and pots of jam and marmalade with jam spoons no less. The 'Tarling's darlings' are in fine fettle. All the musicians plumped for beans and toast. They will be walking behind us today!

Quote this morning – 'Will Kemp - I hate the man'.

Coachloads of blacked-up faces and other Morris people have arrived to give us a good send off. It is quite a nippy day. There is a lot of enthusiasm and well-wishers in this pretty little village. 'Mighty Oak Ale Dancer' is being served at 8.30 am in the square. It has been provided by one of the sides that are with us today. Apparently this rabble will be with us all day and very welcome too. Castle Hedingham and the local Morris sides have certainly welcomed us and done us proud with their hospitality. A cheerful display of molly dancing called *Cross Hand Polka* performed by **Good Easter Molly**.

The villagers are strolling along to the local shop for their newspapers and stopping to watch the dancing and drinking at this early hour of the morning. There is a wonderful feeling of comradeship. Also I think a wonderful feeling of hang-over. It was difficult to leave the Bell last night.

'The Mighty Oak Ale Dancer is 4.5 and is very pleasant.'

Leaving Castle Hedingham to *Hunt the Squirrel*. The first 3 miles have gone well. 3.1 miles in an hour.

Peter talking 'I have just been trying to phone my office because they have been trying for me to go live on the local radio station so I have got my mobile phone and hands-free kit and just about to phone. If they have arranged it I shall be live while dancing.

Howard (who at this moment is driving the support vehicle and taking over the diary while I race back to Great Dunmow with Tom in Bendover to retrieve a missing coat) – 'One frustrating thing about driving is there is beautiful countryside, the weather is nice and I have no opportunities to take photographs. I find that very frustrating. But that's made up for by the fact that I am sitting in a very comfy seat.

I have just found out something quite interesting – the route they are taking from Castle Hedingham to Sudbury is rather a long route. They don't know which route Will Kemp took from Castle Hedingham to Sudbury. They know he went to Sudbury but Steve C. was saying earlier on he was rather pissed off that they are going all this way to Sudbury when they could have taken a much shorter route so I shall find out later why we are taking this longer route. Actually what I said there doesn't quite make sense, we *are* taking the most direct route from Castle Hedingham to Sudbury.

Oops – I nearly ran over Dave just then. He caught his hankie on the bush and I was looking at the map. Good job I looked up when I did or I would have flattened him. Everybody seems to be bearing up remarkably well considering how much in pain they were last night and all the injuries and blisters and Dave's swollen foot. I mean – he is dancing away. Everyone is back to normal. You wouldn't think that these were the same people really.'

(Back again with missing coat)

Quite a steep hill out of Castle Hedingham. The oil-seed rape is looking very healthy on our right as we dance out of the village. This is not doing the people with hay fever any favours. The road at this point is very windy. Dangerous to dance along

Balmer Tyes – First stop at 10.45 am. The roads are quiet.

The Fox – 'Young's Bitter not Young's Special. £1.85. Atmosphere – not much.'

Coffee came with a dainty mint choc wrapped in foil in the saucer. Pity I have given up chocolate for Lent. The coffee was the sort that took ages to drip through a filter.

Bendover has to stay behind in the car park as it has a hole in the tyre and Tom requires assistance to loosen the wheel nuts. He will catch us up later. How many Morris men does it take to change a tyre? – One, all the rest are in the pub. Well, for a very short time, and then you can't see Bendover for enthusiastic car mechanics in bells. But still Tom has to wait for help. The darned wheel nuts will not budge.

I was told that Mark fell out of the top bunk last night. He was on his way to relieve himself of the beer he had drunk and forgot where he was.

All the Morris sides that are joining us on this leg are following the long-distance dancers. There is quite a long file of them. Reaching the town of Sudbury at 11.25 am. It is all downhill here. There are twigs over the pavements. They are being kicked out of the way by the marshals so the dancers do not slip on them. A stone signpost in the grass verge says London 55 miles. The tune has changed going down this really long hill. There are car mechanics to our left and over the road. They have stopped work and come out of the garage to wave and cheer us on. They look a very happy bunch of lads. Sudbury is a pretty town. The houses are painted in a variety of colours. This seems to be the custom in Suffolk. I am told by a local inhabitant that the houses are painted different colours because then the men recognise which house to stagger to after a session at the pub.

Now we have lost our way and asking directions to the town centre from a young woman who is pushing a buggy. We are winding around small side streets of Sudbury. Coming into the town centre. It looks very busy. Stopping at the pub and leaning against the pub wall and stretching calf muscles. The pub is called the Anchor.

'Very very friendly pub. Two pints of beer bought for me by Cambridge Morris Men who are very nice men. I don't know how much it is. IPA and very nice.'

Mark seems to favour the word 'nice' today.

It is clouding over as we dance out of Sudbury to *British Grenadiers*. It looks like rain. I talked that up. It is now starting to rain pretty heavily. This is a residential area with terraced houses and small front gardens and a variety of fences. A fair proportion of the houses on both sides of the road have dogs barking at us through the living room windows. With the local beasties in mind we must watch where we are stepping along this bit of the pavement.

A brief stop to wait for the mini bus to catch us up. Across the road from our brief stop is a road called Abbey Road. The long-distance dancers are having their photograph taken in the well-known Beatles pose strutting across it one behind the other. Steve has a knotted hanky on his head and Peter has wrap-around sun glasses on.

We are dancing through a leafy lane. This is just up the road from where the dogs live, so once more we know to be careful of stepping in any little presents for the rose bushes. The leaves are wet and quite slippery. The boughs are hanging in our path and dripping the rain on to us. It is very pleasant though.

Tom from America hasn't turned up today. I think he is taking his wife back to the airport. I expect he will join us later today or tomorrow.

Coming into Long Melford at 12.50 pm. One of the wenches from Kentwell Hall has come jumping down the road to greet us. She is bouncing up and down and hugging everyone and is in really good cheer. She is flaunting her well-developed cleavage and the men are enjoying the spectacle. It feels good to be greeted heartily after a rather boring stretch of the road. This jollification is keeping our spirits up. She really is buxom though. Her bum roll is swaying and her fox-tail is bobbing. Her rustic skirt has been pinned up to reveal petticoats. Yet more wenches have come to meet us. Even more cuddles and prancing about. John is in his usual place at the front of the procession and the buxom wench has grabbed hold of him and escorted him on his way. He has a huge grin on his face. We have reached the Swan in high spirits and on time at 12.15 pm. A great deal of beer being consumed.

'Another pub where I have had more beer bought for me. It is quite passable Abbott Ale. It should be £2.30 a pint – extremely expensive but it is really nice when it is free. The pub is very full with funny people in there with black faces.'

Leaving the Swan at 13.30 pm to process half a mile up the road and then off to lunch. The wenches are dancing arm in arm with the dancers and swaying their hips outrageously. Up the hill and along by the lovely green with Long Melford Hall on our right hand side. We are stopping off at The Black Lion Coach House where we are departing to have lunch at Kentwell Hall. A good sight to see the long-distance dancers processing along in front of cottages with the host sides dancing along behind. Wenches, black faces, hankies which are all flying in unison. The musicians playing *Lord of the Dance* with gusto in front. The euphonium player is 'oompahing' at the back and I can hear a drum beating. The euphonium player belongs to the side with black faces.

Long Melford – 'processing along in front of the cottages'

The mini bus stopped in the public car park and we are negotiating our way around the puddles and mud that have formed on the long drive leading to the hall. There is an Information Building on the right of the main entrance and **'a really nicely tiled ladies' loos which are clean and smart'** on the left.

Into Kentwell Hall. On the way along the drive leading to the Hall, Mark showed me his arm that has come up into rather a nasty lumpy rash where he skidded and fell into a nettle bush earlier in the day.

The house is gorgeous. It's a lovely old Tudor building and is surrounded by a moat. The brick design on the forecourt is interesting. Apparently it was derelict until 15 years ago when a retired barrister took pity on it and restored it to its full glory. I definitely should like to come back at some time and stroll around at my leisure.

The weather is very blowy outside and the door to the undercroft where the lunch is set out slams very hard every time someone comes in. The room is interesting. Stone pillars dotted here and there. The walls are in the process of being painted with scenes from Tudor and Second World War. Paul Dufficey, who is the artist, is busy working on the end wall as we eat. He is copying the picture from the front of a video box of Laurence Olivier. He explains that the Hall hosts re-enactments and living history of these two periods and this is why he decided to do these particular murals. He tells me that the eldest girl's bedroom is tastefully painted with murals from Beardsley. He has also painted a splendid Chinese room as well. Paul is extremely interested in the 'nine daies wonder' and chattered for a long time about it.

Going upmarket each meal – table cloths and real flower arrangements on the table, wild and rambley with authentic dead leaves.

Leek and potato soup, a variety of rolls and fruit cake is being served by young ladies in a rather touristy food bar setting at the end of the room.

We are leaving Kentwell Hall. Howard seems to be sporting one red knee sock and one green ankle sock. He says it is comfortable and he looks a peculiar sight.

Leaving the lay-by at 3.50 pm. The fiddler from **Kemp's Men**, Gill, has joined us.

Passing 'Avent Naturally' factory and offices. The office workers at the front of the building are hanging out of the windows to wave us on our way. This factory is absolutely out in the middle of the country. Not a pub, shop or post office in sight. Reckon the people who work here have to be very well organised.

4.15 pm. Must be getting to tea time. One of the dancers from **Mzdemeanours** has arrive to dance with us. We are arriving in Cavendish. The wenches are here to meet us. They are still as jolly and playful as ever.

Five Bells at Cavendish at 4.30 pm. Tom from America has joined us. He has been staying with Ann from **Mzdemeanours**. She didn't know him from Adam but heard he was coming to England to take part in the event and offered to put him and his wife Wendy up. Tom will now be joining us for the rest of the way. He is busy having his photograph taken in Olde Worlde England and enjoying every minute of it. He has forgotten his Morris bells. He left them in London so planned to visit Cecil Sharp House and purchase some more. No luck, they haven't got a shop there any more.

A very genteel and wealthy looking gentleman has turned up wearing a green coat. He says he owns Colts Hall, which is about a mile and a half from the pub and where Will Kemp spent three nights on his journey in 1600. He invites us to have a look around and thought it would be splendid if we danced there. Everyone seems keen about this idea but we are dancing to a tight schedule and the next port of call is a brewery that has offered to stay open for us and supply free beer. A hard decision. We are very tempted to visit Colts Hall because this is such an unexpected offer but of course we couldn't pass up the invitation from the brewery. We grovel like crazy and beg the chap to allow us to visit after we have been to the brewery. Yes – that's OK. Yippee!

The Five Bells 'Old Speckled Hen – again I don't know how much it cost because a long-distance dancer bought it for me. Quite a basic pub – not too good décor but passable. Not one to come back to.'

But the view from the front of the pub is very pleasant. A rich green spreads out at the foot of the pub and is surrounded by cottages. No traffic.

As the Morris men perform a rowdy version of *Black Joke* in front of The Five Bells it starts to rain. The badges and feathers from off their bowler hats are flying into the air and scattering around the ground. **The Lords and Ladies Clog Side** dance next. They look very pretty in green skirts, black waistcoats and white blouses but they also look perished with the cold. They also look very happy. A photo call for all the long-distance dancers on Cavendish Green. For a change the photo call included the marshals and support.

Leaving the Five Bells at 5.10 pm. The other sides are still dancing outside the pub and entertaining the crowd. A winding road out of Cavendish. The cars returning from work are building up and the marshals have quite a job to keep the traffic under control. Oh-ahing over the speed bumps on the road.

Arriving in Clare at 5.40 pm. As we turn the corner there is a rider on horse back coming towards us. The horse is becoming a bit skittish because of our hankies so we move slowly on with hankies down. We have arrived at the Globe at 5.55 pm. Another photo call.

Mark – 'Today's lay-by wasn't anywhere near as good as yesterday's lay-by because the hedges are shorter and we had to pee in a field.'

We are directed along the road and arrive at this garage-looking place. It is set back off a very ordinary side road that can be found in any town. The doors have been flung wide open and inside we spy a row of barrels.

Nethergate Brewery –'The owner is an extremely nice chap. I had a little chat with him. Wasn't too keen on the very malty bitter which was 4% but the Nethergate Special which was 4.5% was extremely nice and very enjoyable at the end of the day.'

Bethan, our delicate young musician, all of 20 years old says she is enjoying the piss-up in the brewery and has a full pint of beer in her hand. **Good Easter Molly** are dancing inside the brewery and it is very squashed with the audience so close that there is danger of them becoming part of the dance. However everyone is in good cheer and enjoying the performance. The musicians have climbed the metal open-work stairs to play overhead on the walkway. There is an exceedingly large amount of standing around drinking and being beer connoisseurs here. Crowds of people have arrived out of curiosity and can't believe their luck. A very pleasant time is being had by all.

Gosh our feet ache though and we would like to get showers and something to eat.

Mark 'We stood outside the Cock Inn and we didn't go in! But we did go into the pub next door'. (The Globe)

Moving off with great reluctance from the brewery to Colts Hall. The lady of the house has just returned from a shopping trip to London to buy shoes. In one of the rooms preparations were in evidence for a wedding. She tried to explain about the extensions that had been built on to the old house but there was so much noise and chatter my dictaphone did not pick up what she said. All that can be understood is:

'In 1865 there was a brilliant year for farming around here and all the local farmers put brick fronts on the houses.'

At Colts Hall – Greene King was served and wine for those who preferred it. Mark 'Greene King – 79p a tin. Its exceptionally good and it was very free and that makes it all the better.'

An unknown voice in the crowd – who said it? - 'I have decided that Mark is the closest you will get to an original Morris man. He dances hard, he drinks hard and he still stays standing despite all that is going on. The amount of mileage we are covering he is capable with the best of them and I just am totally jealous really.'

Mark – 'And I'll buy you a pint later.'

After much discussion about routes taken by Kemp and pondering over maps with the gentleman of the house and domestic talk about how to keep such a splendid house tidy with the lady of the house, the dancers leave the kitchen and shake hands with their host. We perform a swift *Highland Mary* in the courtyard. The long-distance dancers have decided that they would like to come back to Colts Hall to stay for the night and sample the comfy beds just as Will Kemp did.

Singing and playing songs on the coach going back to The Globe. A lot of them can be recognised as Sid Kipper songs. They are very funny and everyone joins in the choruses. We have had a very good time today. The support has been absolutely wonderful. Dave S. is so full of cheer that he keeps forgetting the ends of the songs and his poor battered feet.

Back to The Globe. There are sides here to greet us on our return, **Gog-ma-gog**, a young energetic molly side from Cambridge being one of them. They are extremely colourful with a variety of coloured faces, garish tights and tattered mini skirts (yes - the men dancers as well). They also wear some unusual hats. I have met and danced with this side before and have heard them singing. One or two have beautiful voices as they sing for King's College Cambridge.

This is tea-time and we are planning to eat here. The food at The Globe is the usual cheap pub grub.

The long-distance dancers are assembling to dance *Vandals*.

The Globe 'Oh that is very alcoholic – it's a lovely bit of stuff. Tanglefoot which is really delicious. £2. Lovely pub. Shame about all these singers. The beer is marvellous. I am drinking Tanglefoot. It's good.'

Most people seemed to be very inebriated and I couldn't get a lot of sense out of them. I think the free beer at the brewery had a lot to do with it. Everyone is singing and in a very merry mood.

I went off to bed early and left the more energetic members of the side behind. I was told that Mark came back on the mini bus to the youth hostel extremely drunk. Apparently he stripped naked en route but I was not witness to this entertainment as I was tucked up with a cup of tea.

The Fifth Day – Wednesday 25 April 2000

We dance past Father Christmas and meet the best ever landlord and landlady

Morris tunes are being sung in the shower (still only one) this morning and whistled up and down the corridor.

Mark fell out of bed again last night.

Steve says 'When we walked through the lounge of the youth hostel to get to the bedrooms last night there were two youths sprawled across the settees. 'Have you been to a fancy dress party?' they ask.
'No we belong to the circus' replies Steve.

Tarling's Darlings

We get up at 6 o'clock
By half past 9 we're gone
Half an hour to dress and eat
The three hours' brief from John

We must rise up early from our bed
To hear all about the day ahead
But it's such a shame
When it's all in vain
And turns out all wrong
We would like another hour asleep
A bit more time to rest our weary feet
But we have to go
Tarling tells us so
And we must obey John

To the tune of Kemp's Processional

Peter Cole made this song up. He says the scansion needs a bit of initiative to make it fit the tune exactly, but it **can** be done – I tried it in the shower this morning.

Packing up to leave the youth hostel. All glad we have completed more than half way but aware that today is the longest distance.

We are back at Clare again, outside the Globe. **Hinton in the Hedges** are dancing. We are about to start the longest day of the journey. Dr Uid is being tied into his squeeze box and off we go at 9.30 am.

The other dancers have joined on the end of the procession and are dancing with us for the first few miles.

Up the hill on Folly Road. There is a disused windmill in a field to our left - or is it a folly? The cowslips are out in full bloom.

Back onto the awful road surface. The musicians are complaining of the cats eyes which are really difficult to sashay around. These are the really old-fashioned style of cats eyes that stand quite proud off the surface of the road.

Arriving at Hundon at 10.10 am. Nothing eventful has happened so far this morning. The support wagon can be seen in the lay-by ahead.

Bethan is strapping her leg up. She is having problems with her shins. Dr Uid has a lump on his arm where the squeeze box is rubbing.

10.35 am – leaving lay-by to *Hopping Down in Kent*.

Out the other end of Folly Road at 10.50 am. Signpost pointing to Bury St Edmund, 12 miles. A line of tall poplar trees to our right. Trying to count them as we go past but too many – about 200 in all. A farmer is running along the hedgerow in his wellies and woolly hat. He has his camera and is trying to take a photograph. He is puffed out after a few yards and gestures to us about how energetic it all is.

Coming into Stradishall at 11.10 am. The people from Hill Farm have come to wave at their gate. Into lay-by at the Bracken Woodcraft Pine Factory Shop at 11.30 am.

Howard's kit has deteriorated over the course of the event. Today he has a knotted hanky on his head, tee shirt, ankle-length green socks and he has put his army boots back on.

Down a lovely leafy lane with a sharp bend. The little cottages along this route are especially well-kept and pretty.

Further down the road a row of council houses. One of them still has the Christmas decorations fastened to the walls. A faded Father Christmas and snowman perch in the sunshine on the porch and a reindeer is prancing up the side wall.

The pace is still very quick but the dancers have established a rhythm. There is occasional jolly banter and Howard's shells are still very clear. Tom from America has taken up the back marker. He is still going well. His long hair is flying in the wind. He looks a fine strapping man – I think he must have the same stature as the butcher Will Kemp danced with.

Onto the A143 to Bury St Edmunds.

Into Wickhambrook. We are stopping at the Plumbers Arms at 12 noon. Still chatty. Peter enjoys a hug from his wife Ruth who has joined us today.

The beer – 'It's got a good head on it. It's in lovely condition. The conditioning gas is bubbling up inside it but not too much for it to be fizzy. Just about perfect, a little cool perhaps but that is because I am boiling hot. Old Speckled Hen. I don't know how much it was because you bought it for me.'

'Extremely pleasant pub with a wide choice of real ales, Abbott Ale, Greene King, IPA, Old Speckled Hen. They all seem to be kept extremely well. This pub is just so marvellous.'

The landlady is providing us with lunch. We phoned ahead to say we were arriving and she asked us if there was anything we required. We jokingly replied 'free food' and she and her staff have raced around to present us with a scrumptious meal.

A brown gingham table cloth has been draped over the pool table at the end of the room. The landlady has really done us proud. What a feast! We are overwhelmed by the hospitality of these people. Lovely, lovely crusty rolls, freshly grilled sausages, salad, masses of olives and hard-boiled eggs, cheeses, baked potatoes, a selection of quiches freshly baked, potato and leek soup. An absolutely wonderful spread. A mad dash between Bethan, Tim and myself to grab the olives as they are placed on the table. You lot will have to be quick if you wish to sample them.

Some people have gone outside to sell programmes and souvenirs to the small crowd that has gathered to see us.

The landlord and landlady are Jim and Marilyn. Everyone is most appreciative of the effort these people have made to join in the celebration and we have made a mental note to revisit if we are in the area again.

The pub is decorated with hops around the ceiling and cascading down the beams. There is also a profusion of horse brasses. It's a very nice pub. Before we leave I saunter around and look at the numerous photographs on the walls which show the pub in various stages down the ages. They look very interesting but I didn't have the time to sort out the dates.

Dave S. and Dr Uid have a jam session on guitars with Steve joining in with the skiffle tea chest, which have all been found in the corner.

Devil's Dyke Morris are dancing outside.

It will be sad to leave this friendly pub but we must get on our way. The landlord has been given a programme of the Nine Daies Morris which we are all signing as we file out of the door. John Tarling is wandering around the hallways of the pub. He has lost his sense of direction.

Devil's Dyke Morris bid us farewell. They are dancing us out of this fine pub - The Plumbers Arms - one of the nicest pubs we have been to. The landlord and lady accompanied by their little boy and girl are waving us on our way. The little girl looks very pretty in her pink top and leggings.

Catering Dave from **Rumford Morris** is circulating headwear for everybody as the sun is out and we are getting hot. The rest of the dancers and musicians have supplied their own hats - Lichfield Militia hat, fisherman's hat, old ladies' Oxfam hat, cavalier hat, straw hat, knotted hanky.

The musicians strike up *British Grenadiers* and we are on our way. Dancing around the parked cars. We leave at 1.15 pm. Perhaps too much to eat as we have slowed down a bit.

Small Suffolk roads. White lines down the middle so traffic control is difficult. A fine display of scarecrows to our left in a field. One of them is wearing a blue frock. The may flowers have started to bloom and brighten up the landscape. Howard is darting into the hedgerows and picking up pheasant feathers along the route, putting them into his button-hole and sharing them amongst the dancers who are pinning them onto their hats.

Dancing in the sunshine through these pretty Suffolk lanes. A few clouds gathering. All the trees are coming into leaf. A lovely day for a stroll. The traffic is building up behind us and the marshals are doing a terrific job. The dancers are all wiping their brows with their dancing hankies.

Up onto the pavement as there is one provided just at the moment to give the traffic a break.

Coming into Chedburgh and stopping at Marquis of Cornwallis at 2.00 pm. The pain-killers are circulating.

'Although Greene King isn't my favourite pint of beer, IPA acceptable and one of the better pints of IPA I've had. £1.80 a pint. Clean pub – not artificial. Landlord – Jim Harvey. He has made a donation to the Nine Daies Wonder.'

While sipping my glass of wine I have spied a meat draw chalked on the black board. I would have thought because it is Easter weekend that they would have had an Easter egg draw. The lucky winners are:

F/R Beef	1st	Rocky
Leg of Pork	2nd	Dan
O/R Chick	3rd	Skin
S/Steak	4th	Manny
Lamb Chop	5th	Big Pete
Gammon Steak	6th	Speedy
Mince	7th	Rolfe
Sausage	8th	Merry Down

Bacon	9th	Pat J
Liver	10th	Skin

Left the pub at 2.30 pm to *Vandals*. Up onto the footpath again. Double white line down road.

The sheep in the field to our left have all stopped grazing and lifted their heads to see where the sound of the bells are coming from. Bottles of water are being passed down the line of dancers. The sun is so hot. 2.55 pm and Howard's shells still ringing out clear.

The drivers in the cars passing are very friendly. Hooting and waving.

3.15 pm – In the distance we can see green-clad Morris dancers. Green faces and sun glasses dancing in the lay-by. A cup of tea is awaiting us from Catering Dave. A photo call.

Leaving lay-by at 3.50 pm with **Green Dragon** dancing on behind. The passengers in the cars that are passing us now are waving white hankies out of the windows. The support crew have gone on ahead into Bury St Edmunds with a shopping list. Tee shirts, bucket (for soaking feet), film for camera.....

Horringer is a delightful, leafy and tree-lined lane. Some shade for the dancers. Bad bends, traffic not too heavy though. Stop at Horringer Six Bells but the pub is not open.

4.20 pm – on we go to *Saturday Night*. 4.35 pm – a long, slow hill and a beautiful evening.

Entering Bury St Edmunds at 4.50 pm. The sun is shining. A cheer going up from the dancers. At West Suffolk College we meet **Bury Fair Morris**. The Mayor of Bury St Edmunds is here to greet us. A welcome drink of water and loos.

High leaps in *The Valentine* from **Bury Fair**. An extract from Will Kemp's diary is being read out on the steps of the college. Two very pretty ladies from **Bury Fair** are dancing *Kemp's Jig*. Happy greetings from the Norwich sides and an overdosing of hugs and cuddles. **Bury Fair** is a very much liked local side.

Steve vaults all the bollards outside the college as a farewell. Away from the college to the tune of *Bungay Roger* at 5.30 pm. Past the 'Alcohol Free Zone' and going into Bury St Edmunds town centre. Waving of hankies from people hanging from upstairs windows. Into the shopping precinct. **Bury Fair** are dancing a mass *Kemp's Jig*. It is very precise and tight and looks good danced en masse. *The Nutting Girl Jig* is also being performed by a lone dancer dressed in pale blue but I haven't been able to find out who he is. There are not a lot of people around as it is just past closing time. The traffic is homeward bound after a working day. Through built-up area dancing to the *Kemp's Processional*. It's getting quite cool as we dance. Howard has abandoned the shells and is beating the time with a tambourine that has had the cymbals removed. **Bury Fair** following on and smiling and performing the *Processional* in full. They really have taken the event seriously and must have practiced hard. Well it has paid off as they look extremely good.

Into Fornham St Martin at 6.20 pm. Half a dozen children are following the procession. They are not dancing though and trotting behind the ladies of **Bury Fair**. Up 'The Street' and a steady hill into the Wool Pack at 6.35 pm. It smells of chips and vinegar as we enter.

'Abbott Ale - yet another Greene King pub - my least favourite but it's growing on me. Very expensive £11 something for 4 pints. Not very keen on the pub. Wood too new. Is old but spoilt in the past.'

Quote - 'Howard's drum sounds like an old baked bean tin'.

There are old bottles of every shape, size and colour strung to alcoves and around the walls with string. Graham, Treasurer of Nine Daies Wonder, bought us all copies of the local newspaper as there is a lovely picture in it of us dancing past the cottages in Long Melford.

7.00 pm - Away from the Wool Pack to *Hunt the Squirrel*. We are thankful this is the last stretch. Decided to dance on the road as footpath not very good and there is not much traffic about at this time of night. **Bury Fair** have been encouraged to dance the rest of the route with us.

Safety was compromised for The Archers at 7.05 pm (the driver and the scribe are fans of The Archers). The safety lights of the support vehicle were switched off in order to hear the next thrilling instalment of Debbie's wedding and Elizabeth's greed.

Steve is dancing at the back beating the drum. He has a lot of energy left. The ladies from **Bury Fair** are keeping up the pace well and chatting to all the long-distance dancers as they go. There are pheasants strutting across the fields as we come to the end of a long day. Dusk is falling. Coming around the corner the end is in sight. The support vehicles are there to welcome us. We finish at Timworth Hall at 7.40 pm. Howard escorted the two ladies from **Bury Fair** to the place we shall be eating tonight. They went ahead in a car and the rest of the dancers were disappointed as they would have liked to have had them sitting on their knees in the mini bus. Bethan looks very tired.

Tim the support driver says that he has crawled along the road at 3 miles an hour for so long now that it will take him 3 days to get to the shops when he goes home.

Back to the pub with the variety of bottles hanging around the walls. As I make my way through the pub I notice they are strung around every room. David ordered beer for the long-distance dancers before we left earlier so there is a collection of full glasses awaiting us as we arrive. What a kind gesture.

Hageneth Morris is outside the pub to greet us. **Lagabag** have arrived – another well-loved local side.

We are eating at long tables similar to a school dining room. The veggies amongst the side were presented with a ploughman's meal. The rest of the side are enjoying a moist, hot shepherd's pie, which is delicious. I think the veggies are going off to find something a bit more substantial.

The long-distance dancers are enjoying themselves in the beer garden dancing and chatting with **Bury Fair**. As usual when Morris folk meet there is much merriment and comradeship. **Westrefelda Morris** who are a new side are busy booking with **Golden Star** to attend their 21st birthday party next year.

All into the coach again. Tom the American is giving us an American rendition of an English rugby song about the delights of a moose.

Rockland village hall at 10.15 pm. We are waiting around for someone to come along with the key and open up. It is cold. Tired and the thought of blowing up air-beds does not appeal. This will be our home for the next 2 nights. All are tired except for Mark who is champing at the bit to get up to the pub for a swift pint or two before they close. Tim and Steve have decided to keep him company.

'White Hart at Rockland – landlord Tom and barman George are very nice chaps. Nice pint of Adnams - £1.70 a pint. Locals are extremely friendly and chatty but think we were mad. They are all very pleased to see us. Really nice atmosphere .'

There is no fridge in the kitchen of the hall. Catering Dave is exploring the new kitchen that he will be king of for the next few days. He doesn't seems very happy but I am positive that he will do a splendid job. The washing facilities are down to one sink. There is a stage at the end of the hall.

John has chosen to set up his bed at the foot of the stage. Mark has camped on the edge of the stage before he departs to partake of his nightcap so if I were John I would move swiftly in case Mark falls out of bed again.

The Sixth Day – Thursday 26 April 2000

Tea and cake around a green wheelie bin

Drizzly rain but not cold. We are a bit smelly. There is much use of mobile phones. Steve says he will burn his Morris kit after this event, put it in a pot and label it 'A Stupid Idea' and give it to anyone who is thinking of doing this again. He has decided to dress as a Shitwitch molly dancer today with a fetching little red floral crimpalene dress and headscarf. He has left his pigtails and balloons behind as he says they make him too hot. Starting off at 9.45 pm.

Arrive at Great Livermere at 10.10 am. It has stopped raining and is good dancing weather. **Haughley Hoofers** join us here. They are parading with their blue/red/white beribboned banner that is causing them a bit of trouble in the wind. The clomp clomp of their clogs is beating time with the music. They have picked up the rhythm of the dancers quickly Entering Troston at 10.25 am. Stopping at the Bull where the catering wagon and Dave is awaiting us. Dave has his cigar hanging out the side of his mouth as usual. Are they having beer or tea? Just the toilets are open. 'Tea sounds marvellous' says Mark. 'Pardon, can you say that again Mark?' The plastic mugs are being collected to wash as the store is getting low. Leaving the Bull at 10.45 am. Jackets and pullovers are being discarded. There's some powerful muck-spreading going on around here. It clears the tubes.

RAF Honington to our left at 11.10 am. The tune is *Hunt the Squirrel*.

To the Fox pub at 11.20 am. The cloggies did a wonderful *Kemp's Processional* along the route. No flagging. Well recommended. The drummer, Paddy Butcher, is welcomed to play along with the long-distance musicians. His ability to pick up the rhythm of the dancers is exceptional.

'The Fox – absolutely diabolical. No real ales and not even a keg Bitter. On – cider, lager, Guinness.' Mark is drinking Lucozade instead.

Tim managed to rearrange the roadside furniture as he arrived outside the pub. He misjudged the height of the signpost and it has been redesigned.

Haughley Hoofers are putting on a display outside the pub. Very nice dancing. All those watching are commenting on the style and are most impressed. Dr Uid saunters over to Paddy and chats with him about his music.

Away from The Fox to the tune of *Saturday Night* at 11.35 am. **Hageneth Morris** will be our dance partners for the next stretch of the journey. The red speed lines painted on the road are very narrow and stand proud of the road. They are quite painful on the feet.

11.50 am. Up ahead we can see hankies waving in the lay-by at Fakenham Magna. The hankies belong to 3 young lasses who I am told re-enact the witches from *Macbeth* for fun at fêtes and fairs. Howard leaps the grass verge to give the nearest one a kiss. There is a group of women and children at the stile waiting for us to cheer us on our way. Fakenham Magna is a very quiet little village but they are giving us heaps of support. Music changing to *Hopping Down in Kent*. The route is getting boring again. The camber of the road is very steep. We have to adjust our stature and gait to compensate but it is pulling on muscles and we arrive in Euston at 12.20 pm very tired.

There are two horses in a field to our left. The bells and hankies are making them very skittish and they are careering around. One has jumped the fencing and escaped into the next field where it is an unwelcome visitor to the sheep. The other horse is trying to follow but gives up at the fence at each attempt.

Kemp's Processional as we dance to lunch at Euston Sports Club. We have made up 34 minutes and we are now only 6 minutes late.

'IPA yet again. Little bit old and past its best. £1.55 and not worth it. But as this isn't a pub it is a good effort.'

Leaving the Sports Club at 1.15 pm to *The British Grenadiers*. It is threatening to rain but not yet. We are entering 'Norfolk and Good'.

Thetford Road ahead of us is closed to traffic because of bridge repairs. The support crew will have to détour and catch up at the other side of the bridge. Because the road is closed the dancers are dancing in a horizontal line across the road. I wonder if anyone has taken a photograph.

Coming up to two more horses. We have learnt our lesson and dance with hankies down. There are fields of pigs to the right. They seem more interested in eating than watching us going by. A stud farm ahead. Best not frighten them or we might get a large bill.

2.10 pm down Castle Street and over the bridge, past the Bridge Pub and into Thetford to *Lord of the Dance*. A Morris side can be spied ahead waiting for us under the trees. Lovely to see an abundance of buttercups on the green. It is starting to rain and getting blowy. **Peterborough Morris** and **Hageneth** follow us into Thetford. Stopping at the monument of Tom Payne. The long-distance dancers are making their way into the Bell.

'The Bell Hotel – Nice décor. Posh hotel. Very ancient. Old Speckled Hen £2.15 a pint. There were only 3 pints left.

'The loos in the Bell smelt lovely'.

Several of the dancers are being asked for their autograph. Two of the **Peterborough Morris Men** have joined us to escort us out of Thetford. No *Kemp's Jig* is being performed here for some reason that I don't know about. Thetford feels unwelcoming.

The first signposts for Norwich appearing. Dancing through a housing development and industrial estate on rather a main road. Swerving to avoid 3 fat ladies who are not attempting to get out of the way. On to the Croxton Road. A funeral procession is coming towards us on the other side of the road. All hats are being taken off by the long-distance members and marching without waving the hankies and the musicians have stopped playing as a mark of respect.

Croxton at 3.26 pm. A long slog up the hill. Oh! what a beautiful thatched cottage-cum-mansion to our right with a thatched peacock on the roof. People are walking along the route thrusting money through the support vehicle window. We stop at 3.35 pm in a lay-by for a breather. It is cold and miserable. A local inhabitant has invited us to his home for tea and home-made pineapple cake. Although this is an unplanned stop, we could do with some distraction and so we make our way into a relatively new housing development where tea is served in china mugs on trays balanced on green wheelie bins. Other neighbours have come out to serve us tea from large tea pots. They were: David Foreman, Jill Wood and Tom Crow. Howard is drinking his tea with his tambourine on his head. He says it is of more use keeping the rain off him than as a musical instrument as it has gone soggy and out of tune. Dave is encouraged to sing to these good people the 'Hot Tea' song. We all join heartily in the chorus. This small show of kindness has cheered us up no end. Everyone is feeling much more lively and enthusiastic.

Sugden and Nudds (the composers of this song) kindly gave me permission to share it with you all.

Bring Us In Hot Tea

Bring us in no rum, for tha's a drink for sailors
But bring us in hot tea, for that will never fail us

Chorus: *So bring us in hot tea, hot tea, and bring us in hot tea*
That's what the blessed ladies make, so bring us in hot tea

Bring us in no cider, for that will send us reeling
But bring us in hot tea, Earl Grey, Ceylon or Darjeeling

Bring us in no white wine for that don't cure no hot thirst
But bring us in hot tea, and be sure to warm the pot first

Bring us in no schnapps, for they are made with brandy
But bring me in hot tea, and a strainer would be handy

Bring us in no gin, for that was mother's ruin
But bring us in hot tea, and put a lump or two in

Bring us in no home brew, we're not inclined to risk it
But bring us in hot tea, oh, and all right, just one biscuit

We'll drink no beer at Christmas, the good book tells the tale
So bring us in hot tea, for the angels said, 'No ale'.

4.10 pm - We are back on the road and it is raining very hard. Up through a forested area. Most of the trees have initials and hearts and arrows carved on them. We have stopped to cover the squeeze box with a black bin bag as it is raining so hard.

The road stretches for miles ahead in a straight line. There is no traffic in sight and we feel very isolated. Pastures to the left with sheep grazing. Military Firing Range to the right. Tired and flagging at 4.45 pm and trying to keep each other's morale up. Meeting the support vehicle at 4.55 pm in the middle of nowhere. Dancing towards it to *Hopping Down in Kent*.

5.15 pm away from lay-by. Most of the dancers are very sore. The musicians are bearing up well. Bethan's cheeks are very rosy. She is having treatment to her knee and Dr Uid is getting his back massaged. The whole processional is slower today. If the sun came out it might put a skip in our step. It seems to be getting dark quickly. The clouds are racing across the sky. Big black heavy clouds. It isn't wet at the moment but cold. Stop for group photo outside army camp taken by a well-wisher. A smell of bacon in the air.

5.55pm. Hankies down because of horses in field on left. The horses have got their ears pricked up and come over to the fence to see us. Out onto the main road. The traffic has built up and the support van can be seen through the trees round the bend. **Peterborough Morris Men** are here to greet us at 6.05 pm Into the Dog and Partridge 55 minutes late. The pipe and tabor man from **King's Men Morris** is standing outside the pub and looking remarkably like John Bull. His mutton-chop whiskers and round belly make him look a very distinguished man.

'Adnams Ale – extremely nice pub. Getting to end of barrel. Bag Man of The Ring bought all performers a drink – forgot about support. £2 a pint.'

Colin stopped to give a radio interview on the route.

6.30 pm left Dog and Partridge. Spirits up with knowledge only 2 miles to go. It's getting dark now. The cars have their headlights on.

Sign to Gt Hockham at 7.05 pm. Half a mile to go. Gt Hockham at 7.10 pm. **The Peterborough Morris Men** have turned out to meet us in the rain. Stopping on the village green. The landlord of the Eagle supplied free ale. We are looking forward to eating and resting. We leave behind a small crowd of well-wishers dancing *Bonny Green Garters* as we wearily get onto the mini bus to be driven back to the hall.

Into the Eagle. **'Adnams Best and London Pride – best pint all day.'**

Sally (Kemp's descendant) and her family have been following us throughout the day and collecting money and selling programmes. They have done a wonderful job and the collection boxes are heavy.

At the White Hart, 30 steak and kidney pies have been ordered in advance. These are very tasty but unfortunately there is no vegetarian option. The veggies have gone to the Chinese takeaway. Some of the long-distance dancers stay on into the night and dance with **Peterborough Morris Men.**

The Seventh Day, Good Friday – Friday 27 April 2000

We turn into Mr Blobby

At 8.15 am prayers are being said, led by John and Colin. A passage from the Bible is read - time for quiet thought.

Loading up the vehicles again with our rather well-used bedding and creased clothing. Stubble has been developing on chins over this last stage of the journey. The morning is sunny and fresh but the forecast is rain and the clouds are building up. The bananas, courtesy of McCarthy, are the first of the fruit to come to an end. (Mr McCarthy is a fruit and vegetable wholesaler in Norwich who met the Norwich long-distance dancers while they were out practising for the nine daies event. They were looking very tired and he was impressed by their determination. Later in the week Dr Uid received a telephone call from him offering the dancers fresh fruit for the event).

Paul Campbell arrived back again to be with us today to finish the route. He has been missed for the 2 days he had to return to work. Welcome back Paul.

Dancing out of Hockham Magna to *Lord of the Dance* at 9.20 am. A very pretty little village green with quaint cottages around it. To our left is a wonderful copse. The sun is shining through the trees and dappling the dancers as they go past. It's lovely to see wild violets in the hedgerows. Turning right to Stow Bedon at 9.30 am. At 10.00 am we are being overtaken by a tractor as we dance in single file because of the very narrow country lane. All the pink piggies are basking in the sunshine and lifting their heads to watch us as we go by. Some are galloping around the vast field in herds. The pig farmer is standing on top of the sties in his wellies. He is shaking his head in disbelief as we go past.

In a lay-by at Stow Bedon and the time is 10.25 am. Catering Dave has given us a small surprise and produced hot cross buns for our mid-morning break. Isn't it strange how these little thoughtful gestures from Dave bring a smile to weary feet. The farmer has raced across his field to join us in the lay-by and is taking a photograph of us.

'....shaking his head in disbelief as we go past'

Paul Campbell is keeping us cheerful along the road with his silly comments and encouragement. He said that he didn't realise just how far we had danced until he drove here to catch us up.

The **Mayflower Men** have turned up to dance with us.

Coming into Rocklands at 10.40 am. A pretty church to the right with a long gravel path to the door, lined with a row of grave stones on each side. Fresh flowers have been placed on numerous graves. Turning left to Hingham. Signpost telling us to 'Mind the Ducks'. The lanes are very narrow with grass growing in the centre of them and single file for traffic. The pace is still keeping up well. There is a strange-looking house to our left with the roof coming down to ground level and a smattering of sky lights. It is called Roof Lodge. I should love to go inside to see the effect of the architecture from the inside. Turning right onto the Scoulton Road with a signpost stating that Gt Ellingham is shortly coming up. The time is 11.15 am. Hingham 2½ miles but we are turning towards Attleborough and travelling down

Church Road to stop at the village hall. Flags are flying around the village hall, which states in the brick work that it was built in 1871. Balloons are also tied to the gate posts. **Kemp's Men** are already dancing at the back of the hall. Stone's Bitter is immediately being passed around the dancers and crew.

Inside the hall, books and games are being sold and there is a raffle and home made cakes for sale. Hot refreshments are also on sale and the smell wafting about the room is appetising. The walls are festooned with yellow balloons. Programmes for the Nine Daies Morris are being sold. The badges have almost gone and people are encouraged to part with their money for key rings instead. We have turned off the route to visit the hall and will be walking back to the crossroads to continue our dance. One of the **Kemp's Men** is joining us for our dance into Hingham. The hedgerows are scattered with primroses and dandelions. The dancers are spread horizontally across the road as there is no point in trying to keep to one side as the road is so narrow. A very difficult time for the marshals.

12.15 pm – Tedious.
12.25 pm – into Hingham. There is a graveyard to the left. Fresh flowers have been placed on the graves and cars are parked outside for those visiting their departed loved ones on this Good Friday.

Stopping at the White Hart in Hingham. We have two local sides from Norwich here to greet us, the rest of the **Kemp's Men** and **The Golden Star**. As 9 of the long-distance gang belong to these sides there is much hugging and slapping of backs.

The White Hart – **'Abbott Ale at £1.90 a pint. Very nice. Bert bought this drink for me.'**

We have a treat of yoghurt with our sandwiches for lunch. A hard decision which flavour to pick. I don't want strawberry.

Champion the wicker horse from **Golden Star** is being worn by a young lady who is the daughter of a member of the side. Her two sisters are also here and will be walking with the dancers into Wymondham. Their dog is also out for a stroll.

Yvonne, the fiddle player, and Monty have joined us again at Hingham. Yvonne plays for **Fleet Morris** and is in her Morris kit today. It is lovely to see them again.

1.25 pm – leaving Hingham. Champion is coming up the rear. Paul has an Easter Bunny hat on. Two floppy ears are blowing in the wind. He looks so cute and cuddly.

Signpost to Wymondham states 4 miles to go at 2.10 pm. The wind is blowing all the hankies to port side. Paul has changed hat and is sporting a colourful fluorescent wig. This is soon changed for a red, yellow and black smoking cap. He says the wig is too hot under his straw hat.

The road is a weary uphill into Wymondham. A signpost saying 'Drive You Steady Bor! Children'. More buttercups scattered across the graveyards on our left. (Norfolk seems to be full of wild flowers and graveyards). 2.30 pm – stop at Cherry Tree pub. Not open. 2.55 pm – starting off again to *Lord of the Dance*.

Paul is wearing a pair of Mr Blobby glasses. He is also wearing his cheeky smile as normal. Everyone up onto the hedgerow to let cars pass. We are having a short snap of sleety rain and it looks as though the sun is trying to get out again. Yes! I was right - we are steaming nicely. A lot of big pot-holes in the road. Loads of ladybirds on the nettles down this narrow track.

As we dance into Wymondham Paul is wearing this season's fashion of furry teddy on his head. He is handing out Mr Blobby masks for the dancers to wear. This must be the thing nightmares are made of, seeing pink blancmange faces with yellow spots bobbing along. Paul has changed to a Union Jack 2000 felt top hat.

The dancers and musicians are very tired and the marshals are encouraging them along into Wymondham. Paul has changed to a Father Christmas hat and the white fluffy bobble is getting into his eyes.

Great clumps of mistletoe hanging from the trees. An old man on a green sit-up-and-beg bike with a wicker basket on the front has just overtaken us. It all seems so 1940s around here. Paul's Father

Christmas hat has just been changed in favour of a tam o' shanter. How many more hats have he got in his bag?

As we round the bend we can see Wymondham Abbey towering above the trees and looking splendid in the sunshine. At the railway track the station master has come to meet us in his uniform.

Now the long-distance dancers are getting mixed up and lost in the crowd of people that have come to see us. Local sides are lining the route to cheer us on. They are clapping and waving and there is a real carnival atmosphere the closer we are getting to Norwich. Stopping in front of the town cross at 4.00 pm. The chip shop is open and the smell is wafting across the square. I am rather surprised to see the shops open on a Good Friday. Catering Dave is here and cups of tea are waiting for us. The wind is strong and blowing the tea out of the cups.

'The Three Keys – Wherry at £1.90 a pint. Quite a nice pub. Nice reception, friendly people but teenage orientated.'

Golden Star are dancing *Ring of Bells* with loud clashing saucepan lids. I joined in to dance *Saturday Night* with them in my fluorescent jacket. They were very rude and said that it was the first time they had danced with a road sweeper.

Heading out of Wymondham at 4.25 pm. A nice old town but the character has been spoilt by modern ideas.

Milestone – London 101, Norwich 6. A swift break as we visit Kett's Oak tree at 5.10 pm. This is believed to be the place where Kett rallied his troops from Wymondham in 1549. A photo call.

Howard is picking at the hedgerows again and decorating himself with flowers and grasses. *Hopping Down in Kent* at 4.25 pm. Hethersett is half a mile ahead.

Arrive outside the King's Head in Hethersett at 6.45 pm

'King's Head – Marstons Pedigree 4.5%, cost ? Woodford's Wherry 3.7% Session Beer. Atmospheric. Some original features and also some modern décor in keeping. The tiled floor is a bonus.'

'**The ladies loos are very clean and exceptionally nice. They look like the setting for a parlour. They are worth a visit.**'

A nice jig performed by Roger of **Golden Star** to three whistles. A display from **Point Devis** outside this very nice pub. The evening is lovely. Food has been ordered here in advance. **Yateley Morris Men** are here. I wonder if the Highway Horse has made the journey. **Fiddle Sticks** thanked all the marshals for their hard work which was lovely.

The Highway Horse has appeared again! He has taken a fancy to Champion and was last seen chasing him down the road.

'He has taken a fancy to Champion'

The food at the pub was not worth £5 but the catering staff and bar staff are very friendly. Again veggies were not catered for. The beer is flowing freely as the local sides are welcoming the dancers in the best way they know.

7.30 pm – a 15 minute warning to load up the mini bus to take us into Norwich. This will be the final time air-beds will be pumped up. The local members of the long-distance gang are heading home for a long awaited bath. There are only 7 people on the mini bus. The collection bucket has been left in the pub in Hethersett. A swift turn about to pick it up.

Arrived at the Hewett School at 8.20 pm. It is very spacious in the main hall and we are rattling around like peas on a drum.

The King's Head, Hall Road, Norwich – **'Two pints of beer. Both were delicious. The first one was bought for me by John, I bought the second one. I couldn't finish it. A delicious pint of Humpty Dumpty. John had a double rum and blackcurrant. First of all we went off to the Chinese takeaway. We had hot beef curry and sweet and sour vegetable and egg fried rice. It was delicious and huge. John and me went into the pub at about quarter to ten and everybody was already there. We were looking like a couple of old men hobbling. Some people gave up their seats for us and let us sit down which was very nice. The landlord gave us some plates and knives and forks and then we just sat and ate and John told me more about his life in the Morris and what he thinks Morris dancing is all about and what it isn't. Very entertaining.**

There are leaflets and maps on the tables for those people who do not know their way around Norwich.

Howard is anxious to find a dog on wheels. He explains 'Allegedly Will Kemp danced into Norwich pulling a dog on wheels. We must try and find one. It's a bit late now. Perhaps we could sellotape a real one to a skate-board but I guess the Animal Rights people would have something to say about that.'

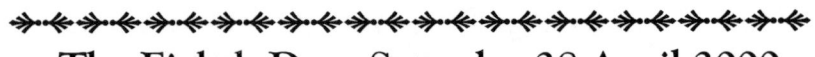

The Eighth Day - Saturday 28 April 2000 the last day

We meet Paul's Little Willie and leap the wall

A nice cup of tea this morning on the last day. The ladies who have come to join their husbands in Norwich are helping to prepare breakfast. Dave has had a bit of a lie-in this morning. He is still busy though, circulating around the tables dishing out badges of his Morris side. A last relaxed chance to sign programmes and Will Kemp's diary and wish each other farewell in writing.

The weather has changed to be warm and sunny. Unfortunately this has encouraged the ants that have come out and they are running around tea cups and in sleeping bags and some people have been bitten rather badly.

Last night as we crawled into our beds most of us were trying to keep our feet suspended in mid air so nothing would touch them. Every time we turned over there is was a reminder of which muscle or bone hurt. Not a lot of sleep.

9.00 am. We are now piling into the mini bus for the last leg of this momentous journey. Feet and blisters have been attended to yet again. Every morning it takes longer and longer to doctor the feet and muscles. Blisters have been burst and new blisters have appeared growing around the blister plasters. Shins are being rubbed and it takes about twenty minutes now to get the legs and feet into some sort of condition to be bearable to put any pressure on them. At the start it only took about five minutes. Ugh this all sounds very grisly. Everyone is in fine cheer.

The weather has become overcast and there are spits of rain but it's not cold. This weather is very changeable. I do hope it keeps fine for our last day.

While driving to Hethersett to start off from where we left last night, there is panic as the scroll from the Lord Mayor of London has gone missing. Have you lot seen where the scroll is? Well you were the last one to wear it. Who's seen the scroll? Help! What the heck will we do now? How can we improvise? Please, please let it be on the other bus.

Energy tablets are being passed around the bus.

On our journey back to Hethersett Peter explains why **Lichfield** wear their rather unusual hats. – 'Because we based our costume on a photograph of the early 1900s and after the original **Lichfield Morris** folded in 1899 (because they only had one musician and he was teetotal and found it difficult to get on with the rest of the side) the tradition was kept up for a while by a team from the local truant school, taught we think by a chap called Mr George who was a member of the 1899 side. In the photographs that we have got of them, they wear hats like we have and that's what we based our costume on. They were probably Army Surplus from the Boer War – that's probably why they had them.'

Mark seems to be powered by drinking beer this week. His nose is definitely red although he assures me it is sun tan. Well you can't be the official beer and pub connoisseur without taking it seriously.

9.20 am – the last leg. Paul Campbell as usual cheering us on. He has a big grin on his face and wearing one of his silly hats. The weather is absolutely appalling. It's not blowing but the puddles are enormous and it's very *very* wet. We are starting from the King's Head at Hethersett. Not much traffic on the roads this morning. It's a Bank Holiday Saturday so there might be a lot of people going to garden centres and into the city to do some shopping later on after an extra hour in bed.

Dr Uid's plumes in his hat are looking decidedly soggy. He has covered up his squeeze box with a brand new black dustbin bag for the special occasion of meeting the Lord Mayor of Norwich. One of the marshals up ahead has skidded over on the wet road. He is limping badly and has got extremely wet. I don't know if he will carry on or not. He is being encouraged by another marshal. It will be sad if he cannot make it after all this effort. Tune – *The British Grenadiers*.

Paul is still trying to keep our spirits up with something that goes like this:

'Who wants to see my little Willie? If you want to see my little Willie you have to shout as loud as you can "Come out little Willie!" '

'Come out little Willie!' Pant pant.

After a while Paul produces a jack doll painted like a Morris man out of a bag.

Willie has got a mate called Bill. He is very old so we have to shout 'Come out of the bag Old Bill, come out of the bag Old Bill.'

Like Paul, Old Bill is a policeman. He has been taking a lot of stick from us, being called 'Plod'. He is the nicest policeman I have ever met. There are a lot of breathless suggestions as to where the jack doll's stick should be shoved into Bill. Paul promises to give us a performance of Willie and Bill later if we are good.

I have just realised that the scroll has been found and I can see it bobbing up and down strapped to Jeff.

The puddles are getting so deep now that the traffic signs painted on the road are covered by muddy puddles and unreadable.

10.00 am A small break to go to the loo behind hedges. Pink dye is running out of Bethan's hat because it is so wet. It is dripping down her arms.

After a brief stop around the hedges the dancing is more brisk. Although the rain has stopped there is a misty wetness in the air. Our clothes are sticking to us and we feel uncomfortable.

Off the main road and leaving the traffic behind. The main road goes into Norwich and we are heading in the direction of Cringleford. There is a signpost for Eaton off to the right. We have a traffic warden to escort on his motor bike into Norwich. The atmosphere is getting exciting.

*(While we were in Clare someone came up to me looking rather irate and asked who had organised the do at the brewery and who had organised free beer. I said 'Well that must have been Paul from the **Thaxted Men** who had gone to all this length to make sure we had free beer at the brewery. – What's your problem?' He said 'Well I would like to shake the hand of a man who has successfully organised a piss up in a brewery.')*

Coming up over the old stone bridge leading into Eaton and on to the pub at the end of the road. Two Norwich Whifflers have come to greet us in the middle of the road and are going to escort us into the City. They are splendid in their red-and-white and blue-and-white pantaloons. Their hats look like pancakes decorated with plumes. It feels wonderful to have these two grand gentlemen clearing the path for us in the same way that Kemp had for him 400 years ago. There are numerous Morris men around dressed in their team's outfits. There seem be quite a crowd of enthusiastic people here to meet us. Roger Green who has travelled from Norway for this event is prancing around resplendent in his skirt and crochet shawl and lovely flowery straw hat. Roger used to dance with **Hageneth**. We are slightly behindschedule as we come into the pub forecourt.

The Red Lion. This is a beautiful old pub. Oak panelled walls, a fire burning at the end of the room and an enormous suit of armour to the side. There is quite a route march to get to the toilets. We have had a wonderful welcome from the crowd of people milling around the pub.

'lovely flowery straw hat'

'The ladies toilets smell fresh and fragrant.'

'Directors - £2.25 a pint. It was quite expensive but an exceptional pint and a very atmospheric pub. A suit of armour in the corner. Beautiful. They welcomed us and opened up especially for us so we could have a pint at half past ten. Excellent.'

The weather has really brightened up at last and it is quite sunny as we come out of the pub. It's coming up for 10.45 am. Off we go to the tune of *Vandals*. The Whifflers are marching in front of the procession and all are admiring their spectacular costumes. John blows the whistle and away we go. The last chunk.

City Centre A11 signpost ahead. Up Blue Bell Road. The music sounds very loud as we go under the fly-over. We are now heading into Norwich. All the men wolf-whistle and call out as two young lady joggers pass us going in the other direction. We are travelling along the bus lane into Norwich. Catering Dave has changed out of civvies and come to greet us in a splendid tail-coat of yellow and red. He looks magnificent. A Cavalier car overtaking us has a pipe and tabor player in the passenger seat. He is playing his pipe while hanging out of the window. He has managed to get out of the car further up the road to join in the procession. He is asked to join the procession at the back as the long-distance musicians are keeping up a regular beat.

Willie is being encouraged again to come out of the bag as we travel down the Newmarket Road. This is a long, long road into Norwich. The traffic warden is stopping at the cross roads to direct the traffic and allow us to cross without being mown down. Round a very busy round about. Apparently this is one of the busiest roads into Norwich. I can see the **Fiddlestick** ladies peeking around the corner to greet us. The bus lane has disappeared and become a cycle track. The traffic warden on the motor-bike is up ahead and seems to be enjoying every moment of his job.

Dr Uid has taken the black dustbin liner off his squeeze box as it has stopped raining and he didn't want to lead the dancers into Norwich with his hands stuffed in a plastic muff. On we go to *Hopping Down In Kent*. It is 11.10 am. The grass verges on the right are covered in purple crocuses. Lovely plush houses behind high walls and bushes. Very wealthy people must live in this area. They are coming out of their houses to wave and hopefully throw us large sums of money. A hip flask is being passed down the line of dancers. A slight détour round the old Norfolk and Norwich Hospital which is being replaced by an all singing all dancing hospital further out of the City. We have been told there is a fair in Chapelfield Gardens this Easter holiday. The dancing was supposed to have stopped in the Gardens. We will be going on to the Assembly Rooms instead.

Chapelfield Gardens are ahead. We can see the old City walls surrounding them. Travelling left down the underpass. The Assembly Rooms are just the other side of the Gardens. Stopping here by the underpass for John to tell us the sequence of events when we enter the City walls. Coming up for 11.30 am. *Kemp's Processional* is being played. This is the grand finale. We have been told there are numerous sides of Morris dancers dotted around the City.

Dancing through Chapelfield Gardens and past the fair that is squeezed to one side. On through the car park of Rowntree-Mackintosh which has been closed down for a number of years. The plan is to build a splendid complex of shops, flats and offices in its place when they finally pull the old factory down. The beautiful church of St Peter Mancroft on the left. Huge blue cranes above us dotting the sky. They are on a building site just over the road from the Assembly Rooms. The City library burnt down some years ago and is being rebuilt. The City Hall clock reads 11.35 am. We are turning right at the end of our journey into the forecourt of the Assembly Rooms.

Champion the wicker horse has escaped the passion of the Highway Horse and come out to greet us. A lot of the Morris sides who have escorted and hosted us along the way have turned up with warm welcomes. Mark has already got a pint in his hand although we have only just stopped. Sally Stevens is here as well.

There must be many Morris sides represented here today. Everything and everyone is so colourful.

The Assembly Rooms –

'It tastes like Adnams. I don't know what it is. One of the Peterborough Men had it waiting. The instant we stopped dancing he thrust it into my hand and it was well deserved. The Assembly Rooms is an absolutely beautiful building. There was a bit of a fire here and they have rebuilt it. It was a marvellous place to stop instead of having to go through Chapelfield Gardens where there was a fun fair. The traffic warden en route was power-crazed and thoroughly enjoyed himself - he was brilliant.'

Ladies and gentlemen in Elizabethan custom are standing around the entrance to the Assembly Rooms. They look very sumptuous and in keeping with this splendid house. **Hoxne Hundred** are putting on a display by the fountains. A mass photo call of all the long-distance dancers, musicians and support team who have completed the entire route. The drum is beating and the **Hoxne Hundred** are now performing a garland dance.

The Elizabethan group are the next side to dance - genteel with dipping and bowing. Lovely atmosphere. The Highway Horse has just arrived. It is amusing the crowd and it is lovely to see him again.

We are meeting up at 1.30 pm on the man-size chess board in Chapelfield Gardens to process to the City Hall for a presentation of the scroll to the Lord Mayor of Norwich. As I hobble out of the forecourt I am told by an ex-Navy man (my dad) that I should have put my feet in potash before I started the journey to harden them up. A bit late now. Apparently this is the practice in the Army.

Someone has told Mark (our good beer guide) that if he hadn't smoked so much he would have been able to go further. I think he has done pretty well leaping and skipping and bouncing for all these miles from London. He probably would have gone on to John O' Groats if he didn't smoke.

Another display of Elizabethan dancing from this beautiful dance group. Now off to Norwich market to buy chips on the way to The Art Centre where several of us are meeting up.

There is a band playing outside City Hall as we walk past on our way to lunch. I suppose this is all part of the day's celebrations and welcoming us back to Norwich. The band is The Sally Army. They are very good and playing some rather unusual tunes.

To the Art Centre in Norwich. A swift pint before we all assemble again on the chess board in the Gardens. The Art Centre is an old church that has been revamped. It has been very tastefully done. Extra staff have been employed at the bar and they have put on food for us which was prepared in bulk so it is cheap. Huge great burgers with salad dripping out of the sides and very substantial and filling.

Some of the other members of the team have gone sight-seeing around Norwich and getting chips from the market.

The Art Centre – **'Cider – puts hairs on your chest – lovely. Someone bought it for me so I haven't a clue how much it was. It's very nice and cheap in here. £1.20 a pint for the beer. Nice and light, nothing heavy. Smashing. Mansfield? IPA. The red wine is nice and fruity.'**

The two bar men were talking in the Art Centre and one said 'What's all this about then?' 'Oh some of them have danced up from London to Norwich' He said 'Didn't anybody tell them there was a bus every two hours?'

Paul is telling the company all about his Willie and how he collects money from people who have come to see him. He is giving graphic details about the performance.

Bethan the musician has just spilt the remainder of her pint into her lap. She is wearing my spare britches so I am not best pleased. I lent them to her to come into Norwich so she could look respectable. She has been wearing black leggings for the last few days. Not very in keeping with the tradition. I shall charge her for having these dry cleaned.

Bethan, Dr Uid, the Scribe and Tom have pooled their money that is left over from the last 8 days. It is being tipped out onto the table top to see how much they have left for a booze-up.

Going towards the check board. The sun has come out and it is wonderful now.

Through the fair, passing the candyfloss stall and swing chairs, and arriving to where the wooden carving of Will Kemp is being worked. There is a crowd gathered around the carving, watching the man at work. It is very unusual and exactly right for the occasion. Morris dancers and musicians are inspecting the carving and nodding and smiling. It is well worth a visit before the vandals get to it with their spray paint.

Sally and her family are here talking to the sculptor.

Kemp's Men dragon, they call him Cyril, has just arrived. His design is based on Snap, the dragon of Norwich. A lot of

'Very unusual and just right for the occasion'

colourful Morris people chatting in groups. A carnival atmosphere.
I can see one of **Belchamp Morris Men** who was with us at Castle Hedingham talking to Mark. *The Jig* is now being played by David Jackson the pipe and tabor man. There are sides dancing in spots around the park. Wonderful headgear worn by some of the men. There are flowers around bowler hats. All can be seen leaping into the air and bobbing around. Over to the left I can see the **Golden Star Morris** performing. They look lively. Their red socks and black britches stand out sharply against the lush green of the bushes. We meet one of the **Belchamp Men** and he hasn't painted his face black but we recognise him. He has met up with one of the long-distance dancers and they have been drinking together in the pub.

Howard and Mark are dancing with **The Golden Star Morris**. John is dancing the *Kemp's Jig* to the playing of David Jackson. John is considerably sprightly considering he has just come all the way from London. David looks swell in his outfit of top hat and tails. He has side whiskers. His appearance reminds me of Mr Bumble or John Bull. A well-larded belly.

Coming up for 2.00 pm. The Highway Horse has had rather too much to drink. He is ambling and rambling everywhere. He looks very unsteady on his feet. The Billericay Badger has arrived. He is chasing the Highway Horse around the park and through the trees. The processional has started out of Chapelfield Gardens and on their way to meet the Mayor. All are being led by the Whifflers. The *Kemp's Processional* is being played yet again. Numerous sides are joining on the end. We are heading down the very busy shopping area of St Stephen's Street in Norwich. The traffic has stopped because we are taking up the entire road. All the shoppers have come out of the shops to see us. Some of them seem surprised. The pig's bladder is in full swing being brandished by Dave of the **Rumford Morris Men** in his splendid tail-coat. Passing Boots the chemist. I don't think we shall be such frequent customers anymore. The Whiffler ahead is waving his sword and hat and clearing the way for us to pass by. The market stalls are to our left hand side as we parade past their rows of striped tarpaulins. There are crowds of people here. The flower stalls and fruit and veg. stalls look enticing. Smoke is coming out of the chimney pots of the chippy stalls.

The local sides are dancing behind the long-distance dancers, **Kemp's Men, Golden Star** with their banner and Champion, **Fiddlesticks, Hoxne Hundred** carrying their garlands, the **Weavers** and then a long line of Morris sides and individual Morris people who are representing their side chatting and dancing the *Kemp's Processional* and really making merry. **The Peterborough Morris Men** have now joined us. They seemed to have been delayed by the crowd. **Devil's Dyke** has been delayed also. It really is difficult to dance through the crowd. I can see two members of **Bury Fair** dancing by the Guild Hall. The wonderful Elizabethan dancers are here as well. There is cheering and clapping from the crowd. A local man told me that when he saw the dancers arrive at the City he felt it was uplifting for Norfolk men. There was such a buzz in the air that he felt quite emotional.

It is sunny and everyone is extremely hot. The long-distance dancers, musicians and support crew are assembling on the steps of the City Hall for a photo call. The television crews are here too. We are ahead of schedule so some Morris sides have been requested to dance and entertain the crowd while we await the City Crier. A mass *William and Nancy* is being performed. The animals of various sides including the **Kemp's** dragon have gathered to one side. They seem to be a friendly little gang, bowing and nodding to each other. **Hoxne Hundred** are about to dance. **Peterborough Men** are dancing the *Lollipop Man* accompanied by the pipe and tabor and a drum. The *Will Kemp Processional* is being danced by the ladies of the Elizabethan group. They are holding hands in a long line and dipping and curtsying. It looks very different when danced by the Morris. Their costumes are made of bold, coloured fabric, rich in braiding. They are being accompanied by three pipe and tabor players. One is wearing rags, one is the John Bull chap and the other is one of the Whifflers. **Fiddlesticks** are giving a vigorous dance display. There is a huge crowd gathered from the foot of the City Hall steps, down the pavement and across the road. The last time I saw a crowd of this size at the City Hall was when the citizens of Norwich gathered to see the year 2000 in.

Ahead of us poking above the top of the striped canopies of Norwich market and through the Davey Place shops can be seen Norwich castle on the hill. It has been closed for refurbishment until April 2001. The outside walls have been sandblasted and it looks very clean. There is polythene sheeting over the battlements and it looks as if it is wearing a headscarf.

Norwich seems to be in the process of relocating and rebuilding and replacing most of the old established buildings. I wonder how many of these will still be left for the next Morris dancers to recognise in 400 years time.

The Mayor in his pristine red and black robes with a tri-cornered hat and black plume is standing on the top step of the City Hall. His grand chain of office is shining in the sunlight. His wife is standing beside him looking very pretty for this occasion. She looks as though she is really enjoying herself. A big smile. John has gone up the City Hall steps to be introduced to the Mayor.

Four of the long distance dancers are sliding down the handrail of the City Hall and landing in the crowd. It looks quite dangerous.

2.30 pm. The City Crier can be seen running up the hill and past the Guild Hall. He is resplendent in his ruffles, red jacket, black breechers and tri-cornered hat.

'*Oyez, oyez! The Right Worshipful, The Lord Mayor of Norwich, in the name of the City Council of Norwich bids the warmest of welcomes to the Nine Daies Morris, to the dancers and the musicians who have danced and played all the way from the City Of London, and their support team, and to the dancers of many dance teams who have joined them along the route and have come to Norwich today to celebrate the ending of the dance. And now a dance by* **Kemp's Men**. *God save the Queen.*' Applause.

'*Oyez, oyez we have gathered here today to honour William Kemp the extraordinary Elizabethan actor and clown who in his own day was famous throughout England and Europe and the finest comedian of his time, and who in 1600 undertook by wager to dance from London to Norwich in nine days, a feat which he accomplished with great gusto and popular applause.*

'Good old Will!' is being shouted from the crowd. Much applause.

'*He took with him a scroll from the Lord Mayor of London to the Lord Mayor of Norwich. In similar tradition, the dancers of the Nine Daies Morris have brought a scroll from the present Lord Mayor of London. A dancer will now perform the Kemp's Jig after which the scroll will be presented to the Lord Mayor. God save the Queen.'*

Mark, one of the long-distance dancers, has been requested to do the Jig. The music is being piped and drummed. He has stamped his roll up out on the steps of the City Hall and is being encouraged to leap high. The performance was described as 'an interesting version and unique display of the Jig.'

Colin is reading to the crowd an excerpt from Kemp's diary of his entry into Norwich.

The Mayor: *'We have just had a celebration of Will Kemp's famous dance. The re-enactment has been completed within eight days by, I understand, a dozen or so bold dancers including one from America who has done the whole route. They have been escorted by teams. Kemp of course had a bet to do the distance in nine days. Those were spread over four weeks. We therefore must congratulate them for such an historic and more intense re-enactment.'*
Applause.

'Well done to you all for your efforts. Can I now ask the City Crier to read from the scroll.'

The City Crier now reads out the scroll.

> From The Right Honourable,
> The Lord Mayor of London, Alderman Clive Allartin, OBE
> to The Right Worshipful, The Lord Mayor of Norwich,
> Councillor Doug Underwood

Greetings, on the occasion of the four hundredth anniversary of the exploits of William Kemp, Elizabethan clown and actor, whose Morris dance from the City of London to the City of Norwich in nine days during Lent became famous as 'The Nine Daies Wonder'
During this journey, he carried greetings from my predecessor to yours, bringing together our two great cities in a single, splendid exploit of endurance and entertainment.
His feat is commemorated in this millennial year by dancers from those Morris sides whose names are listed below and who come from our two cities and beyond.

They are setting out on the last Saturday in Lent from the vicinity of the Mansion House in the City of London, arriving on Saturday in Easter week at City Hall in the City of Norwich.

(Here follows a list of participating sides)

As Lord Mayor of London, I hereby take great pleasure in renewing this historic link between our respective civic corporations and desire you to convey our respectful greetings to the members of your ancient corporation.

Motor bikes go past at this point. The City Crier has to stop for a while. Everybody takes off their hats to 'God save the Queen'.
Golden Star dance at the bottom of the City Hall steps as the long-distance dancers are leading the way to the church wall at the Maddermarket at 3.15 pm.

The Morris dancers leap the wall from the inside and over into the alley way. The wall is very high. Grave stones are now lining the wall so it would be impossible to jump from the alley into the churchyard. I am not sure which way Kemp jumped but I am sure it couldn't have been into the churchyard if the height was the same as it is now. Even the gate is a good four feet off the ground with pillars on either side.

A mighty cheer is heard up and down the narrow alleyway as each dancer and musician and some of the support crew leap the wall. The space is very restricted and only a very few members of the public can witness the leaping. Morris sides squeeze in as best they can but only the lucky few have managed to get to the front.

I am astonished they have managed the leap with their sore feet and aching muscles but all the pain seems to have disappeared with the excitement of the finale. A few of the other Morris sides are attempting to jump the wall as well. Mark has been tossed back over the wall into the graveyard by some boisterous Morris men. *The Jig* is being danced again by Steve.

A plaque on the wall of the Maddermarket Theatre which is opposite to the church wall is being unveiled by the Lord Mayor. This is dedicated to Will Kemp commemorating his dance in 1600. There have been other plaques attached to the church wall in the past but these have all disappeared over the years. This plaque has been well and truly fixed. The Lord Mayor has been encouraged to leap the wall.

There is loud applauding as he comes flying over. I must say he is a jolly sort of Mayor.

It is now 4.50 pm and we are in St Andrew's Tavern relaxing and drinking beer, Morris side networking and exchanging addresses.

Dave of **Belchamp Morris** is asking for details of the **Golden Star** 21st birthday party. His address is being written on a beer mat.

Talking to Paul. – 'The **Mayflower Morris Men** decided to have their animal as a badger. This is Bill the Badger from Billericay. There is a children's book by an author who I can't remember called *Bobwitch and Bagderman* and it's for seven and eight-year-olds and about five years ago it was number one in the children's book selling list. Now recently wherever Bill the Badger goes there are lots of children who not only adore the badger but shout 'Badgerman, Badgerman!' Badgerman in his books apparently is quite a magical and ancient creature who collects acorns. A charming and sweet story – there we go. I do believe in animal circles that possessing arms gives one the ability to speak because most Morris animals are mute. There is no utterance to be heard from anyone.

He continued.

'When we finally reached Norwich I was reduced to tears. I couldn't believe that we didn't have another three and a half miles to do. I kept asking people "Is this the end? Have we stopped? Are we here now?" '

The musician, Dr Uid is auctioning his black plastic bag that covered the squeeze box for a few miles into the City. It is still wet from the rain. He has given 10p to Paul Campbell to take it away. It has been decided to auction it on at the reunion later in the year.

At St Andrew's Tavern. Much merry-making, much friendship making. Kemp's Caper Brew special for the occasion will be served at the ceilidh tonight. Most of us didn't have time to go back to the school to get changed for the feast and ceilidh tonight which starts at 6 o'clock. We will have to attend in Morris kit without having a shower but as we have been in Morris kit all week this will feel normal. Things are being gathered together to walk across the road to the feast and the ceilidh. Tickets have been given to us to say we are participants.

Coming up for 6.00 pm as we sit in St Andrew's Hall which is very impressive. It was once a church. There is an enormous organ at the front. The tables are all set out down each side of the room. People are already here and wearing their finery. We feel quite stinky and crumpled at the top end of the room. The hall is filling up quite rapidly and the ceilidh should be spectacular later in the night. People are queuing up for the beer, which is in a barrel just beside the long-distance dancers tables. Trust our group to get a space right by the beer table. Bartram's Brewery. We believe the beer is free. John is sporting a green and red jester's hat. Is this his best bib and tucker? More members of the public are turning up. The Molly from **Hageneth** has just arrived in regular Morris kit. He is hardly recognisable out of his skirt and his snazzy little straw hat. His blue eyes are twinkling as brightly as ever. He says he would like to return to this country because he misses the Morris and the way of life that we have here. He misses the people and the foolishness of us all.

The beer is not free – **it is £2 a pint. Described as 'not bad'.**

Looking around the hall I can see Sally and her family who seem to take up an entire table. They have turned out in bulk to congratulate us.

The presentations are being given to the whole-route dancers and musicians. A rather splendid pewter tankard with Will Kemp engraved on the front and their names underneath this. Now a photo call for all the dancers and musicians after the presentation. People are lining up to be able to take their photograph and they are having to 'say cheese' for heck of a long time.

A few speeches are being made. The acoustics in the hall made it impossible for the tape recorder to pick up and I lost this piece of the event. (The usual about thanking organisers and bouquets given to Colin and John's wives.)

We intend to drink and make merry before the ceilidh starts. The bread rolls are being passed down the table. Most of the people who have received a tankard are drinking beer from them. First course – Chinese chicken, pâté, fruit salad. It is very palatable. A plate full of beef and mushroom or pork chop, veggies have an option of vegetable bake or cannelloni. We queue up for our meal at long trestle tables at the side of the hall. The service is like school dinners. There is a second helping if needed. Pudding – cheesecake, trifle, meringue, mousse, fresh fruit salad or chocolate cake - all with loads of cream. Folk music is being played while we eat. The food tables are being cleared away in a hurry. Second helpings of the pudding are being scooted away and Tom leaps across the room to rescue the meringue. Members of the public who have not managed to obtain tickets for the feast are getting restless at the doors and wanting to join in the fun. A toast to Will Kemp.

Banners hang from the stone archways. Large pictures of dignitaries are hanging in between the leaded glass windows. There is not a tremendous amount of stained glass. The stage at the top of the hall under the enormous organ is set up for the ceilidh later tonight. Some photographs that have been taken during the route have already been developed and are being sold for 60p each.

The ceilidh band, called The Washday Miracles, has started while we are still drinking our coffee. Friends, family, well-wishers are all gathered together now and the dance floor is heaving. Not a lot of room to manoeuvre. Most of the long-distance dancers are watching the dancing with their feet up. The younger men who danced the whole route are joining in the dancing. A really good atmosphere. Signing lots of books for each other and members of the public. E-mail numbers and telephone numbers are being exchanged. A lot of friendships have been forged over the last 8 days. This will never be forgotten by those who have taken part. A reunion is being planned for later in the year back in Castle Hedingham which I think was voted the prettiest village and best pub that we visited on our journey.

Colin introduces the team of the 8 days members to everyone and then introduced the Kemp's descendants and a hearty round of applause was given.

The all-route dancers left the ceilidh at about 11.00pm - back to the floor of the school. They will be packing up their kit tomorrow.

Thoughts of the Nine Daies Wonder

Dave Stewart: 'I don't really know. That was all right. A fun week. Knackered now.'

Paul Mower: 'At 10 minutes past four this morning I woke up in excruciating agony and couldn't actually move to get out of bed. I realised that I must have cracked a rib yesterday when I fell off the kerb while we were coming into Norwich.'

Tim Sercombe: 'I have had an absolutely marvellous time. I think the organisation was second to none. The company was phenomenal especially The Scribe. She was lovely. We have had a great time and it is sad that it has all come to an end. If it didn't come to an end it would get boring wouldn't it? We have to go away and do something completely different now. Here's to the next time.'

John Tarling: 'I just think it was a great event. It put everyone who took part into a great comradeship and put in touch people who hadn't been in touch before. It broke down some barriers as well.'

Howard Templeton: 'Gor blimey. You can't just throw me into the deep end like this. I would do it all again. I loved every minute of it. Says he now not in any pain whatsoever.'

Mark Jones: 'The whole event was absolutely brilliant. It's really nice to get back to Norwich. A bit of an anti climax now.'

Steve Conneely: 'I would never do it again. No never ever. I would find something better to do.'

Thomas Baxter: 'After the first day I dropped out of the event. I didn't get back until Tuesday evening. It's been absolutely wonderful. Sometimes I felt a little bit of a freak, you know, being American, but I soon felt like one of the dancers. It's really been a privilege to be part of this and one of this group. I think I am quite numbed by the roads because everything is so cool here. Different flowers. I don't know how the farmers manage. Something of a kind of vision to go to a far away place and go through some physical trials. It's been a lot of fun apart from the blisters and the sore knee. I feel a lot more in touch with the Morris dancing. I can understand the hanky movements now and stuff. It takes some of the weight off of the knees which is quite helpful. I am hoping to bring back a few more dancers. The *Lichfield Hat Dance* is one I must learn. One thing that has amazed me above anything else is the fact that we are part of a Morris community here. The people and the dancers seem very familiar even though they are thousands of miles away. Just like the Morris dancers back home. Just wonderful.'

Jeffrey Evans: 'Well we successfully completed the challenge I think. We are all pretty sore and aching after it all but well worth doing.'

Paul Campbell: 'What I was there for... it was wonderful. The bits I missed I really missed.'

Peter Cole: 'Yeah I think twenty-four hours afterwards the memory of the pain and sort of having to drive myself on through all that has sort of gone and the thing that really sticks in my mind above all else is the camaraderie along the way, within the people doing it and with the people outside as well really because we were sort of egged along by people cheering us and stuff like that, but the thing that really sticks in my mind is the sort of team spirit within the people doing it. Everyone who was involved along the way really.

David Marr: 'My final thoughts on this is a very excellent adventure. Very good fun and if I was to do it again I would do a bit more in the way of preparation for this especially in the way of looking after the feet and getting them nice and toughened up at the back of the ankles. But I think we gelled together well as a team.'

Peter Salt 'I would walk further in front and make sure the wind was blowing in the right direction otherwise you would get the contents of my stomach twenty-four hours later.'

Also available from the Larks Press

Kemps nine daies wonder

Will Kemp's own story of his original dance
from London to Norwich
in 1600 A.D.

Price £2.70 (postage free)